SWAMI VIVEKANANDA
tells STORIES

A collection of stories told by Swami Vivekananda

Compiled and edited by
Swami Atmashraddhananda

Advaita Ashrama
(PUBLICATION DEPARTMENT)
5 DEHI ENTALLY ROAD • KOLKATA 700 014

Published by
Swami Bodhasarananda
Adhyaksha, Advaita Ashrama
Mayavati, Champawat, Uttarakhand, Himalayas
from its Publication Department, Kolkata
Email: mail@advaitaashrama.org
Website: www.advaitaashrama.org

ISBN 978-81-7505-397-7

Printed in India at
Trio Process
Kolkata 700 014

PUBLISHER'S NOTE

As readers of Swami Vivekananda's works may recall, Swamiji was a wonderful storyteller. His talks and writings are interspersed with numerous anecdotes and illustrations. Some of these are well-known, while others are not, but they are all relevant and thought-provoking, revealing his profound knowledge of human nature—its potential and its limitations. This collection contains most of the stories from his nine-volume Complete Works published by us.

These stories were serialized from January 2005 to January 2010, under various titles, in The Vedanta Kesari, the English monthly published by Sri Ramakrishna Math, Chennai. The idea of publishing them in this manner was well received and welcomed by one and all. Some were even surprised that Vivekananda had told so many stories. And as all these stories are in Swamiji's own words, there is an additional charm and value to them.

The 106 stories contained in this volume have been classified under 10 headings. Some are just a paragraph, while others go on for several pages, but all are sure to give readers fresh insights. The compilation and arrangement has been done by Swami Atmashraddhananda, the present editor of The Vedanta Kesari. Sri Mahendra C. Zinzuvadia has created the beautiful line drawings for the book, for which we are very grateful. When the world is

celebrating the 150th birth anniversary of Swami Vivekananda, we are sure this book will be widely read.

01 May 2013   Publisher

CONTENTS

ATTACHMENT OR NON-ATTACHMENT

MYRIAD FORMS OF LOVE

HAPPINESS

MAYA

MIND AND CONCENTRATION

FAITH AND SACRIFICE

WOMEN OF INDIA

ATTITUDE

SELF-REALIZATION

MISCELLANEOUS

SCIENCE AND RELIGION

1. Human Understanding

All men, so-called, are not yet really human beings. Every one has to judge of this world through his own mind. The higher understanding is extremely difficult. The concrete is more real to most people than the abstract.

As an illustration of this, a story is told of two men in Bombay—one a Hindu and the other a Jain—who were playing chess in the house of a rich merchant of Bombay. The house was near the sea, the game long; the ebb and flow of the tide under the balcony where they sat attracted the attention of the players. One explained it by a legend that the gods in their play threw the water into a great pit and then threw it out again. The other said: 'No, the gods draw it up to the top of a high mountain to use it, and then when they have done with it, they throw it down again. A young student present began to laugh at them and said, 'Do you not know that the attraction of the moon causes the tides?' At this, both men turned on him in a fury and inquired if he thought they were fools. Did he suppose that they believed the moon had any ropes to pull up the tides, or that it could reach so far? They utterly refused to accept any such foolish explanation.

At this juncture the host entered the room and was appealed to by both parties. He was an educated man and of course knew the truth, but seeing plainly the impossibility of making the chess-players understand it, he made a sign to the student and then proceeded to give an explanation of the tides that proved eminently satisfactory to his ignorant hearers. 'You must know', he told them, 'that afar off in the middle of the ocean, there is a huge mountain of sponge—you have both seen sponge, and know what I mean. This mountain of sponge absorbs a great deal of the water and then the sea falls; by and by the gods come down and dance on the mountain and their weight squeezes all the water out and the sea rises again. This, gentlemen, is the cause of the tides, and you can easily see for yourselves how reasonable and simple is this explanation.'

The two men who ridiculed the power of the moon to cause the tides, found nothing incredible in a mountain of sponge, danced upon by the gods! The gods were real to them, and they had actually seen sponge; what was more likely than their joint effect upon the sea! (CW, 8:13-14)

2. Two Approaches

In America there was a great agnostic, a very noble man, a very good man, and a very fine speaker. He lectured on religion, which he said was of no use; why bother our heads about other worlds? He employed this simile; we have an orange here, and we want to squeeze all the juice out of it.

I met him once and said, 'I agree with you entirely. I have some fruit, and I too want to squeeze out the juice. Our difference lies in the choice of the fruit. You want an orange, and I prefer a mango. You think it is enough to live here and eat and drink and have a little scientific knowledge; but you have no right to say that

that will suit all tastes. Such a conception is nothing to me. If I had only to learn how an apple falls to the ground, or how an electric current shakes my nerves, I would commit suicide. I want to understand the heart of things, the very kernel itself. Your study is the manifestation of life, mine is life itself. My philosophy says you must know that and drive out from your mind all thoughts of heaven and hell and all other superstitions, even though they exist in the same sense that this world exists. I must know the heart of this life, its very essence, what it is, not only how it works and what are its manifestations. I want the why of everything. I leave the how to children. As one of your countrymen said, 'While I am smoking a cigarette, if I were to write a book, it would be the science of the cigarette.'

It is good and great to be scientific, God bless them in their search; but when a man says that is all, he is talking foolishly, not caring to know the raison d'être of life, never studying existence itself. I may argue that all your knowledge is nonsense, without a basis. You are studying the manifestations of life, and when I ask you what life is, you say you do not know. You are welcome to your study, but leave me to mine.' (CW, 2:186-187)

3. Not a drop of Water

Many years ago, I visited a great sage of our own country, a very holy man. We talked of our revealed book, the Vedas, of your Bible, of the Koran, and of revealed books in general. At the close of our talk, this good man asked me to go to the table and take up a book; it was a book which, among other things, contained a forecast of the rainfall during the year.

The sage said, 'Read that.'

And I read out the quantity of rain that was to fall.

He said, 'Now take the book and squeeze it.' I did so and he said, 'Why, my boy, not a drop of water comes out. Until the water comes out, it is all book, book. So until your religion makes you realise God, it is useless. He who only studies books for religion reminds one of the fable of the ass which carried a heavy load of sugar on its back, but did not know the sweetness of it.' (CW, 1:326)

4. Where were these rishis?

About fourteen hundred years before Christ, there flourished in India a great philosopher, Patanjali by name. He collected all the facts, evidences, and researches in psychology and took advantage of all the experiences accumulated in the past. Remember, this world is very old; it was not created two or three thousand years ago. It is taught here in the West that society began eighteen hundred years ago, with the New Testament. Before that there was no society. That may be true with regard to the West, but it is not true as regards the whole world.

Often, while I was lecturing in London, a very intellectual and intelligent friend of mine would argue with me, and one day after using all his weapons against me, he suddenly exclaimed, 'But why did not your rishis come to England to teach us?'

I replied, 'Because there was no England to come to. Would they preach to the forests?'

'Fifty years ago,' said Ingersoll to me, 'you would have been hanged in this country if you had come to preach. You would have been burnt alive or you would have been stoned out of the villages.'

So there is nothing unreasonable in the supposition that civilisation existed fourteen hundred years before Christ. (CW, 2:27)

5. Story of the Deluge

This is the one fact that comes out of every scripture and of every mythology that the man that is, is a degeneration of what he was. This is the kernel of truth within the story of Adam's fall in the Jewish scripture. This is again and again repeated in the scriptures of the Hindus; the dream of a period which they call the Age of Truth, when no man died unless he wished to die, when he could keep his body as long as he liked, and his mind was pure and strong. There was no evil and no misery; and the present age is a corruption of that state of perfection. Side by side with this, we find the story of the deluge everywhere. That story itself is a proof that this present age is held to be a corruption of a former age by every religion. It went on becoming more and more corrupt until the deluge swept away a large portion of mankind, and again the ascending series began. It is going up slowly again to reach once more the early state of purity. You are all aware of the story of the deluge in the Old Testament. The same story was current among the ancient Babylonians, the Egyptians, the Chinese, and the Hindus.

Manu, a great ancient sage, was praying on the bank of the Ganga, when a little minnow came to him for protection, and he put it into a pot of water he had before him. 'What do you want?' asked Manu.

The little minnow declared he was pursued by a bigger fish and wanted protection. Manu carried the little fish to his home, and in the morning he had become as big as the pot and said, 'I cannot live in this pot any longer'.

Manu put him in a tank, and the next day he was as big as the tank and declared he could not live there any more. So Manu had to take him to a river, and in the morning the fish filled the river.

Then Manu put him in the ocean, and he declared, 'Manu, I am the Creator of the universe. I have taken this form to come and warn you that I will deluge the world. You build an ark and in it put a pair of every kind of animal, and let your family enter the ark, and there will project out of the water my horn. Fasten the ark to it; and when the deluge subsides, come out and people the earth.' So the world was deluged, and Manu saved his own family and two of every kind of animal and seeds of every plant. When the deluge subsided, he came and peopled the world; and we are called 'man', because we are the progeny of Manu. (CW, 2:72-73)

6. Until You Know God

The sense universe is, as it were, only one portion, one bit of that infinite spiritual universe projected into the plane of sense consciousness. How can this little bit of projection be explained, be understood, without knowing that which is beyond? It is said of Socrates that one day while lecturing at Athens, he met a Brahmin who had travelled into Greece, and Socrates told the Brahmin that the greatest study for mankind is man.

The Brahmin sharply retorted: 'How can you know man until you know God?' This God, this eternally Unknowable, or Absolute, or Infinite, or without name—you may call Him by what name you like—is the rationale, the only explanation, the raison d'etre of that which is known and knowable, this present life. (CW, 3:2)

7. Freedom—the Only Condition of Growth

Buddha died at a ripe old age. I remember a friend of mine, a great American scientist, who was fond of reading his life. He did not like the death of Buddha, because he was not crucified. What a false idea! For a man to be great he must be murdered! Such ideas never prevailed in India. This great Buddha travelled all over India, denouncing her gods and even the God of the universe, and yet he lived to a good old age. For eighty years he lived, and had converted half the country.

Then, there were the Charvakas, who preached horrible things, the most rank, undisguised materialism, such as in the nineteenth century they dare not openly preach. These Charvakas were allowed to preach from temple to temple, and city to city, that religion was all nonsense, that it was priestcraft, that the Vedas were the words and writings of fools, rogues, and demons, and that there was neither God nor an eternal soul. If there was a soul, why did it not come back after death drawn by the love of wife and child? Their idea was that if there was a soul it must still love after death, and want good things to eat and nice dress. Yet no one hurt these Charvakas.

Thus India has always had this magnificent idea of religious freedom, and you must remember that freedom is the first condition of growth. What you do not make free, will never grow. The idea that you can make others grow and help their growth, that you can direct and guide them, always retaining for yourself the freedom of the teacher, is nonsense, a dangerous lie which has retarded the growth of millions and millions of human beings in this world. Let men have the light of liberty. That is the only condition of growth. (CW, 2:114-115)

8. 'I Want Religion'

A disciple went to his master and said to him, 'Sir, I want religion.' The master looked at the young man, and did not speak, but only smiled. The young man came every day, and insisted that he wanted religion. But the old man knew better than the young man.

One day, when it was very hot, he asked the young man to go to the river with him and take a plunge. The young man plunged in, and the old man followed him and held the young man down under the water by force. After the young man had struggled for a while, he let him go and asked him what he wanted most while he was under the water. 'A breath of air', the disciple answered. 'Do you want God in that way? If you do, you will get Him in a moment,' said the master. Until you have that thirst, that desire, you cannot get religion, however you may struggle with your intellect, or your books, or your forms. Until that thirst is awakened in you, you are no better than any atheist.'

A great sage used to say, 'Suppose there is a thief in a room, and somehow he comes to know that there is a vast mass of gold in the next room, and that there is only a thin partition between the two rooms. What would be the condition of that thief? He would be sleepless, he would not be able to eat or do anything. His whole mind would be on getting that gold. Do you mean to say that, if all these people really believe that the mine of happiness, of Blessedness, or Glory were here, they would act as they do in the world, without trying to get God?'

As soon as a man begins to believe there is a God, he becomes mad with longing to get to Him. Others may go their way, but as soon as a man is sure that there is a much higher life than that which

he is leading here, as soon as he feels sure that the senses are not all, that this limited, material body is as nothing compared with the immortal, eternal, undying bliss of the Self, he becomes mad until he finds out this bliss for himself. And this madness, this thirst, this mania, is what is called the 'awakening' to religion, and when that has come, a man is beginning to be religious. (CW, 2:45-46)

9. The Salt Doll

The case of ordinary Jivas is like that of the salt-doll which, attempting to sound the depths of the ocean, melted into it. Do you see? The sum and substance of it is—you have only got to know that you are Eternal Brahman. (CW, 7: 142)

VASANAS OR HABITS

10. The Bugle Sound

To worship is inherent in every man's nature; only the highest philosophy can rise to pure abstraction. So man will ever personify his God in order to worship Him. This is very good, as long as the symbol, be it what it may, is worshipped as a symbol of the Divinity behind and not in and for itself. Above all, we need to free ourselves from the superstition of believing because 'it is in the books'. To try to make everything—science, religion, philosophy, and all—conform to what any book says, is a most horrible tyranny. Book-worship is the worst form of idolatry.

There was once a stag, proud and free, and he talked in a lordly fashion to his child, 'Look at me,

see my powerful horns! With one thrust I can kill a man; it is a fine thing to be a stag!' Just then the sound of the huntsman's bugle was heard in the distance, and the stag precipitately fled, followed by his wondering child. When they had reached a place of safety, he inquired, 'Why do you fly before man, O my father, when you are so strong and brave?' The stag answered, 'My child, I know I am strong and powerful, but when I hear that sound, something seizes me and makes me fly whether I will or no.' So with us. We hear the 'bugle sound' of the laws laid down in the books, habits and old superstitions lay hold of us;

and before we know it, we are fast bound and forget our real nature which is freedom. (CW, 8:33-34)

11. 'Thou art That'

There was once a Hindu queen, who so much desired that all her children should attain freedom in this life that she herself took all the care of them; and as she rocked them to sleep, she sang always the one song to them—'Tat tvam asi, Tat tvam asi' ('That thou art, That thou art'). Three of them became sannyasins, but the fourth was taken away to be brought up elsewhere to become a king. As he was leaving home, the mother gave him a piece of paper which he was to read when he grew to manhood. On that piece of paper was written, 'God alone is true. All else is false. The soul never kills or is killed. Live alone or in the company of holy ones.' When the young prince read this, he too at once renounced the world and became a sannyasin. (CW, 7:89,90)

12. Bondage of Nature

[Nature is] like the Frenchman who had invited an English friend and told him of his old wines in the cellar. He called for a bottle of old wine. It was so beautiful, and the light sparkled inside like a piece of gold. His butler poured out a glass, and the Englishman quietly drank it. The butler had brought in a bottle of castor oil! We are drinking castor oil all the time; we cannot help it. (CW, 7:434)

13. The Old Chinaman

All the misery we have is of our own choosing; such is our nature. The old Chinaman, who having been kept in prison for sixty years was released on the

coronation of a new emperor, exclaimed, when he came out, that he could not live; he must go back to his horrible dungeon among the rats and mice; he could not bear the light. So he asked them to kill him or send him back to the prison, and he was sent back. Exactly similar is the condition of all men. We run headlong after all sorts of misery, and are unwilling to be freed from them. Every day we run after pleasure, and before we reach it, we find it is gone, it has slipped through our fingers. Still we do not cease from our mad pursuit, but on and on we go, blinded fools that we are. (CW, 1:408)

14. The Story of Vilvamangala

This is a story from one of the books of India, called 'Lives of Saints'. There was a young man, a Brahmin by birth, in a certain village. The man fell in love with a bad woman in another village. There was a big river between the two villages, and this man, every day, used to go to that girl, crossing this river in a ferry boat.

Now, one day he had to perform the obsequies of his father, and so, although he was longing, almost dying to go to the girl, he could not. The ceremonies had to be performed, and all those things had to be undergone; it is absolutely necessary in Hindu society. He was fretting and fuming and all that, but could not help it. At last the ceremony ended, and night came, and with the night, a tremendous howling storm arose. The rain was pouring down, and the river was lashed into gigantic waves. It was very dangerous to cross. Yet he went to the bank of the river. There was no ferry boat. The ferrymen were afraid to cross, but he would go; his heart was becoming mad with love for the girl, so he would go. There was a log floating down, and he got that, and with the help of it, crossed the river, and getting to the other side dragged the log up, threw it on the bank, and went to the house.

The doors were closed. He knocked at the door, but the wind was howling, and nobody heard him. So he went round the walls and at last found what he thought to be a rope, hanging from the wall. He clutched at it, saying to himself, 'Oh, my love has left a rope for me to climb.' By the help of that rope he climbed over the wall, got to the other side, missed his footing, and fell, and the noise aroused the inmates of the house, and the girl came out and found the man there in a faint.

She revived him, and noticing that he was smelling very unpleasantly, she said, 'What is the matter with you? Why this stench on your body? How did you come into the house?' He said, 'Why, did not my love put that rope there?' She smiled, and said, 'What love? We are for money, and do you think that I let down a rope for you, fool that you are? How did you cross the river?' 'Why, I got hold of a log of wood.' 'Let us go and see,' said the girl. The rope was a cobra, a tremendously poisonous serpent, whose least touch is death. It had its head in a hole, and was getting in when the man caught hold of its tail, and he thought it was a rope. The madness of love made him do it. When the serpent has its head in its hole, and its body out, and you catch hold of it, it will not let its head come out; so the man climbed up by it, but the force of the pull killed the serpent. 'Where did you get the log?' 'It was floating down the river.' It was a festering dead body; the stream had washed it down and that he took for a log, which explained why he had such an unpleasant odour.

The woman looked at him and said, 'I never believed in love; we never do; but, if this is not love, the Lord have mercy on me. We do not know what love is. But, my friend, why do you give that heart to a woman like me? Why do you not give it to God? You will be perfect.' It was a thunderbolt to the man's brain. He got a glimpse of the beyond for a moment. 'Is there a God?' 'Yes, yes, my friend, there is,' said the woman. And the man walked on, went into a forest, began to weep and pray. 'I want Thee, Oh Lord! This tide of my love cannot find a receptacle in little human beings. I want to love where this mighty river of my love can go, the ocean of love; this rushing tremendous river of my love cannot enter into little pools, it wants the infinite ocean. Thou art there; come Thou to me.' So he remained there for years.

After years he thought he had succeeded, he became a sannyasin and he came into the cities. One day he was sitting on the bank of a river, at one of the bathing places, and a beautiful young girl, the wife of a merchant of the city, with her servant, came and passed the place. The old man was again up in him, the beautiful face again attracted him. The yogi looked and looked, stood up and followed the girl to her home. Presently the husband came by, and seeing the sannyasin in the yellow garb he said to him, 'Come in, sir, what can I do for you?' The yogi said, 'I will ask you a terrible thing.' 'Ask anything, sir, I am a Grihastha (householder), and anything that one asks I am ready to give.' 'I want to see your wife.' The man said, 'Lord, what is this! Well, I am pure, and my wife is pure, and the Lord is a protection to all. Welcome; come in sir.' He came in, and the husband introduced him to his wife. 'What can I do for you?' asked the lady. He looked and looked, and then said, 'Mother, will you give me two pins from your hair?' 'Here they are.' He thrust them into his two eyes saying, 'Get away, you rascals! Henceforth no fleshy things for you. If you are to see, see the Shepherd of the groves of Vrindaban with the eyes of the soul. Those are all the eyes you have.' So he went back into the forest. There again he wept and wept and wept. It was all that great flow of love in the man that was struggling to get at the truth, and at last he succeeded; he gave his soul, the river of his love, the right direction, and it came to the Shepherd. The story goes that he saw God in the form of Krishna.

Then, for once, he was sorry that he had lost his eyes, and that he could only have the internal vision. He wrote some beautiful poems of love. In all Sanskrit books, the writers first of all salute their Gurus. So he saluted that girl as his first Guru. (CW, 1: 485-88)

3

15. Lingering Hope

There was a great king in ancient India who was once asked four questions, of which one was: 'What is the most wonderful thing in the world?'

'Hope,' was the answer.

This is the most wonderful thing. Day and night we see people dying around us, and yet we think we shall not die; we never think that we shall die, or that we shall suffer. Each man thinks that success will be his, hoping against hope, against all odds, against all mathematical reasoning. Nobody is ever really happy here. If a man be wealthy and have plenty to eat, his digestion is out of order, and he cannot eat. If a man's digestion be good, and he have the digestive power of a cormorant, he has nothing to put into his mouth. If he be rich, he has no children. If he be

hungry and poor, he has a whole regiment of children, and does not know what to do with them. Why is it so? Because happiness and misery are the obverse and reverse of the same coin; he who takes happiness, must take misery also. We all have this foolish idea that we can have happiness without misery, and it has taken such possession of us that we have no control over the senses. (CW, 1:409-410)

16. Lion and Sheep

Nothing is baser than calling our brother a sinner. A lioness once fell upon a flock of sheep and killed a lamb. A sheep found a very young lion, and it followed her, and she gave it suck, and it grew up with the sheep and learned to eat grass like a sheep. One day an old lion saw the sheep lion and tried to get it away from the sheep, but it ran away as he approached. The big lion waited till he caught the sheep lion alone, and he seized it and carried it to a clear pool of water and said, 'You are not a sheep, but a lion; look at your picture in the water.'

The sheep lion, seeing its picture reflected from the water, said, 'I am a lion and not a sheep.'

Let us not think we are sheep, but be lions, and don't bleat and eat grass like a sheep. (CW, 7:420-421)

17. Fisherwomen in a Florist's House

But be not like certain fisherwomen, who, caught in a storm on their way home from market, took refuge in the house of a florist. They were lodged for the night in a room next to the garden where the air was full of the fragrance of flowers. In vain did they try to rest, until one of their number suggested that they wet their fishy baskets and place them near their heads. Then they all fell into a sound sleep.

The world is our fish basket, we must not depend upon it for enjoyment. Those who do are the Tamasas or the bound. Then there are the Rajasas or the egotistical, who talk always about 'I', 'I'. They do good work sometimes and may become spiritual. But the highest are the Sattvikas, the introspective, those who live only in the Self. These three qualities, Tamas, Rajas, and Sattva (idleness, activity, and illumination), are in everyone, and different ones predominate at different times. (CW, 7:12)

ATTACHMENT OR NON-ATTACHMENT

18. Non-attachment

Neither seek nor avoid, take what comes. It is liberty to be affected by nothing; do not merely endure, be unattached. Remember the story of the bull. A mosquito sat long on the horn of a certain bull. Then his conscience troubled him, and he said, 'Mr. Bull, I have been sitting here a long time, perhaps I annoy you. I am sorry, I will go away.' But the bull replied, 'Oh no, not at all! Bring your whole family and live on my horn; what can you do to me?' (CW, 7:14)

19. True Contentment

'Yes, Yes!' he reiterated. 'You Western folk want action! You cannot yet perceive the poetry of every common little incident in life! What beauty could be greater than that of the story of the young mother coming to Buddha with her dead boy? Or the incident of the goats? You see the Great Renunciation was not new in India! ... But after Nirvana, look at the poetry!

'It is a wet night, and he comes to the cowherd's hut and gathers in to the wall under the dripping eaves. The rain is pouring down and the wind rising.

'Within, the cowherd catches a glimpse of a face through the window and thinks, 'Ha, ha! Yellow garb! Stay there! It's good enough for you!' And then he begins to sing.

"My cattle are housed, and the fire burns bright. My wife is safe, and my babes sleep sweet! Therefore ye may rain, if ye will, O clouds, tonight!'

'And the Buddha answers from without, 'My mind is controlled: my senses are all gathered in; my heart firm. Therefore ye may rain, if ye will, O clouds, tonight!'

'Again the cowherd: 'The fields are reaped, and the hay is fast in the barn. The stream is full, and the roads are firm. Therefore ye may rain, if ye will, O clouds, tonight.'

'And so it goes on, till at last the cowherd rises, in contrition and wonder, and becomes a disciple.

'Or what would be more beautiful than the barber's story?

'The Blessed One passed by my house, my house—the Barber's!

'I ran, but He turned and awaited me,
Awaited me—the Barber!
'I said, 'May I speak, O Lord, with Thee?'
'And He said 'Yes!'
'Yes!' to me—the Barber!
'And I said, 'Is Nirvana for such as I?'
'And He said 'Yes!'
Even for me—the Barber!
'And I said, 'May I follow after Thee?'
'And He said, 'Oh yes!'
Even I—the Barber!
'And I said, 'May I stay, O Lord, near Thee?'
'And He said, 'Thou mayest!'
Even to me—the poor Barber!' (CW, 8:272-273)

20. From Gross to Subtle

There was once a minister to a great king. He fell into disgrace. The king, as a punishment, ordered him to be shut up in the top of a very high tower. This was done, and the minister was left there to perish. He had a faithful wife, however, who came to the tower at night and called to her husband at the top to know what she could do to help him. He told her to return to the tower the following night and bring with her a long rope, some stout twine, pack thread, silken thread, a beetle, and a little honey.

Wondering much, the good wife obeyed her husband, and brought him the desired articles. The husband directed her to attach the silken thread firmly to the beetle, then to smear its horns with a drop of honey, and to set it free on the wall of the tower, with its head pointing upwards. She obeyed all these instructions, and the beetle started on its long journey. Smelling the honey ahead it slowly crept onwards, in the hope of reaching the honey, until at last it reached to top of the tower, when the minister grasped the beetle, and got possession of the silken thread. He told his wife to tie the other end to the pack thread, and after he had drawn up the pack thread, he repeated the process with the stout twine, and lastly with the rope.

Then the rest was easy. The minister descended from the tower by means of the rope, and made his escape. In this body of ours the breath motion is the 'silken thread'; by laying hold of and learning to control it we grasp the pack thread of the nerve currents, and from these the stout twine of our thoughts, and lastly the rope of Prana, controlling which we reach freedom. (CW, 1:143-144)

21. Neither Good Nor Evil

It [the world] is a great gymnasium in which you and I, and millions of souls must come and get exercises, and make ourselves strong and perfect. This is what it is for. Not that God could not make a perfect universe; not that He could not help the misery of the world. You remember the story of the young lady and the clergyman, who were both looking at the moon through the telescope, and found the moon spots.

And the clergyman said, 'I am sure they are the spires of some churches.'

'Nonsense,' said the young lady, 'I am sure they are the young lovers kissing each other.'

So we are doing with this world. When we are inside, we think we are seeing the inside. According to the plane of existence in which we are, we see the universe. Fire in the kitchen is neither good nor bad. When it cooks a meal for you, you bless the fire, and say, 'How good it is!'

And when it burns your finger, you say, 'What a nuisance it is!'

It would be equally correct and logical to say: This universe is neither good nor evil. The world is the world, and will be always so. (CW, 4:207)

22. Story of a Young sannyasin

A young sannyasin went to a forest; there he meditated, worshipped, and practised yoga for a long time. After years of hard work and practice, he was one day sitting under a tree, when some dry leaves fell upon his head. He looked up and saw a crow and a crane fighting on the top of the tree, which made him very angry. He said, 'What! Dare you throw these dry leaves upon my head!' As with these words he angrily glanced at them, a flash of fire went out of his head—such was the yogi's power—and burnt the birds to ashes. He was very glad, almost overjoyed at this development of power—he could burn the crow and the crane by a look.

After a time he had to go to the town to beg his bread. He went, stood at a door, and said, 'Mother, give me food.' A voice came from inside the house, 'Wait a little, my son.' The young man thought, 'You wretched woman, how dare you make me wait! You do not know my power yet.' While he was thinking thus the voice came again: 'Boy, don't be thinking too much of yourself. Here is neither crow nor crane.' He was astonished; still he had to wait.

At last the woman came, and he fell at her feet and said, 'Mother, how did you know that?' She said, 'My boy, I do not know your yoga or your practices. I am a common everyday woman. I made you wait because my husband

is ill, and I was nursing him. All my life I have struggled to do my duty. When I was unmarried, I did my duty to my parents; now that I am married, I do my duty to my husband; that is all the yoga I practise. But by doing my duty I have become illumined; thus I could read your thoughts and know what you had done in the forest. If you want to know something higher than this, go to the market of such and such a town where you will find a Vyadha [butcher] who will tell you something that you will be very glad to learn.'

The sannyasin thought, 'Why should I go to that town and to a Vyadha?' But after what he had seen, his mind opened a little, so he went. When he came near the town, he found the market and there saw, at a distance, a big fat Vyadha cutting meat with big knives, talking and bargaining with different people.

The young man said, 'Lord help me! Is this the man from whom I am going to learn? He is the incarnation of a demon, if he is anything.' In the meantime this man looked up and said, 'O Swami, did that lady send you here? Take a seat until I have done my business.' The sannyasin thought, 'What comes to me here?' He took his seat; the man went on with his work, and after he had finished he took his money and said to the sannyasin, 'Come sir, come to my home.'

On reaching home the Vyadha gave him a seat, saying, 'Wait here,' and went into the house. He then washed his old father and mother, fed them, and did all he could to please them, after which he came to the sannyasin and said, 'Now, sir, you have come here to see me; what can I do for you?'

The sannyasin asked him a few questions about soul and about God, and the Vyadha gave him a lecture which forms a part of the Mahabharata, called the Vyadha-Gita. It contains one of the highest flights of the Vedanta. When the Vyadha finished his teaching, the sannyasin felt astonished. He said, 'Why are you in that body? With such knowledge as yours why are you in a Vyadha's body, and doing such filthy, ugly work?'

'My son,' replied the Vyadha, 'no duty is ugly, no duty is impure. My birth placed me in these circumstances and environments. In my boyhood I learnt the trade; I am unattached, and I try to do my duty well. I try to do my duty as a householder, and I try to do all I can to make my father and mother happy. I neither know your yoga, nor have I become a sannyasin, nor did I go out of the world into a forest; nevertheless, all that you have heard and seen has come to me through the unattached doing of the duty which belongs to my position.' (CW 1:68-70)

23. 'Getting Nearer to the Lord'

B less men when they revile you. Think how much good they are doing you; they can only hurt themselves. Go where people hate you, let them thrash the ego out of you, and you will get nearer to the Lord. Like the mother-monkey, we hug our 'baby', the world, as long as we can, but at last when we are driven to put it under our feet and step on it* then we are ready to come to God. (CW, 7:15)

[*The mother-monkey is very fond of her young, but if an iron plate is heated under her feet and it becomes unbearable, she throws down the baby and stands on it to save herself.]

24. The Story of Jada Bharata

There was a great monarch named Bharata. The land which is called India by foreigners is known to her children as Bharata Varsha. Now, it is enjoined on every Hindu when he becomes old, to give up all worldly pursuits—to leave the cares of the world, its wealth, happiness, and enjoyments to his son—and retire into the forest, there to meditate upon the Self which is the only reality in him, and thus break the bonds which bind him to life. King or priest, peasant or servant, man or woman, none is exempt from this duty; for all the duties of the householder—of the son, the brother, the husband, the father, the wife, the daughter, the mother, the sister—are but preparations towards that one stage, when all the bonds which bind the soul to matter are severed asunder for ever.

The great king Bharata in his old age gave over his throne to his son, and retired into the forest. He who had been ruler over millions and millions of subjects, who had lived in marble palaces, inlaid with gold and silver, who had drunk out of jewelled cups—this king built a little cottage with his own hands, made of reeds and grass, on the banks of a river in the Himalayan forests. There he lived on roots and wild herbs, collected by his own hands, and constantly meditated upon Him who is always present in the soul of man.

Days, months, and years passed. One day, a deer came to drink water near by where the royal sage was meditating. At the same moment, a lion roared at a little distance off. The deer was so terrified that she, without satisfying her thirst, made a big jump to cross the river. The deer was with young, and this extreme exertion and sudden fright made her give birth to a little fawn, and immediately after she fell dead. The fawn fell into the water and was being carried rapidly away by the foaming stream, when it caught the eyes of the king. The king rose from his position of meditation and rescuing the fawn from the water, took it to his cottage, made a fire, and with care and attention fondled the little thing back to life.

Then the kindly sage took the fawn under his protection, bringing it up on soft grass and fruits. The fawn thrived under the paternal care of the retired monarch, and grew into a beautiful deer. Then, he whose mind had been strong enough to break away from lifelong attachment to power, position, and family, became attached to the deer which he had saved from the stream. As he became fonder and fonder of the deer, the less and less he could concentrate his mind upon the Lord. When the deer went out to graze in the forest, if it were late in returning, the mind of the royal sage would become anxious and worried. He would think, 'Perhaps my little one has been attacked by some tiger—or perhaps some other danger has befallen it; otherwise, why is it late?'

Some years passed in this way, but one day death came, and the royal sage laid himself down to die. But his mind, instead of being intent upon the Self, was thinking about the deer; and with his eyes fixed upon the sad looks of his beloved deer, his soul left the body. As the result of this, in the next birth he was born as a deer. But no Karma is lost, and all the great and good deeds done by him as a king and sage bore their fruit. This deer was a born Jatismara, and remembered his past birth, though he was bereft of speech and living in an animal body. He always left his companions and was instinctively drawn to graze near hermitages where oblations were offered and the Upanishads were preached.

After the usual years of a deer's life had been spent, it died and was next born as the youngest son of a rich Brahmin. And in that life also, he remembered all his past, and even in his childhood was determined no more to get entangled in the good and evil of life. The child, as it grew up, was strong and healthy, but would not speak a word, and lived as one inert and insane, for fear of getting mixed up with worldly affairs. His thoughts were always on the Infinite, and he lived only to wear out his past Prarabdha Karma.

In course of time the father died, and the sons divided the property among themselves; and thinking that the youngest was a dumb, good-for-nothing man, they seized his share. Their charity, however, extended only so far as to give him enough food to live upon. The wives of the brothers were often very harsh to him, putting him to do all the hard work; and if he was unable to do everything they wanted, they would treat him very unkindly. But he showed neither vexation nor fear, and neither did he speak a word. When they persecuted him very much, he would stroll out of the house and sit under a tree, by the hour, until their wrath was appeased, and then he would quietly go home again.

One day, when the wives of the brothers had treated him with more than usual unkindness, Bharata went out of the house, seated himself under the shadow of a tree and rested. Now it happened that the king of the country was passing by, carried in a palanquin on the shoulders of bearers. One of the bearers had unexpectedly fallen ill, and so his attendants were looking about for a man to replace him.

They came upon Bharata seated under a tree; and seeing he was a strong young man, they asked him if he would take the place of the sick man in bearing the king's palanquin. But Bharata did not reply. Seeing that he was so able-bodied, the king's servants caught hold of him and placed the pole on his shoulders. Without speaking a word, Bharata went on. Very soon after this, the king remarked that the palanquin was not being evenly carried, and looking out of the palanquin addressed the new bearer, saying 'Fool, rest a while; if thy shoulders pain thee, rest a while.'

Then Bharata laying the pole of the palanquin down, opened his lips for the first time in his life, and spoke, 'Whom dost thou, O King, call a fool? Whom dost thou ask to lay down the palanquin? Who dost thou say is weary? Whom dost thou address as `thou'? If thou meanest, O King, by the word `thee' this mass of flesh, it is composed of the same matter as thine; it is unconscious, and it knoweth no weariness, it knoweth no pain. If it is the mind, the mind is the same as thine; it is universal. But if the word `thee' is applied to something beyond that, then it is the Self, the Reality in me, which is the same as in thee, and it is the One in the universe. Dost thou mean, O King, that the Self can ever be weary, that It can ever be tired, that It can ever be hurt? I did not want, O King—this body did not want—to trample upon the poor worms crawling on the road, and therefore, in trying to avoid them, the palanquin moved unevenly. But the Self was never tired; It was never weak; It never bore the pole of the palanquin: for It is omnipotent and omnipresent.' And so he dwelt eloquently on the nature of the soul, and on the highest knowledge, etc.

The king, who was proud of his learning, knowledge, and philosophy, alighted from the palanquin, and fell at the feet of Bharata, saying, 'I ask thy pardon, O mighty one, I did not know that thou wast a sage, when I asked thee to carry me.' Bharata blessed him and departed. He then resumed the even tenor of his previous life. When Bharata left the body, he was freed for ever from the bondage of birth. (CW, 4:111-114)

25. Why We Disagree

'A frog lived in a well. It had lived there for a long time. It was born there and brought up there, and yet was a little, small frog. Of course the evolutionists were not there to tell us whether the frog lost its eyes or not, but, for our story's sake, we must take it for granted that it had eyes, and that it every day cleansed the waters of all the worms and bacilli that lived in it, with an energy that would give credit to our modern bacteriologists. In this way it went on and became a little sleek and fat—perhaps as much so as myself. Well, one day another frog that lived in the sea, came and fell into the well.

'Whence are you from?"

'I am from the sea."

'The sea? How big is that? Is it as big as my well?' And he took a leap from one side of the well to the other.

'My friend,' says the frog of the sea, `how do you compare the sea with your little well?"

Then the frog took another leap and asked; `Is your sea so big?"

'What nonsense you speak to compare the sea with your well."

'Well, then,' said the frog of the well, `nothing can be bigger than my well; there can be nothing bigger than this; this fellow is a liar, so turn him out." (CW, 7:290)

MYRIAD FORMS OF LOVE

26. Love for God

One beautiful story he [Swami Vivekananda] told was of a man whose wife reproached him with his troubles, reviled him because of the success of others, and recounted to him all his failures. 'Is this what your God has done for you', she said to him, 'after you have served Him so many years?' Then the man answered, 'Am I a trader in religion? Look at the mountain. What does it do for me, or what have I done for it? And yet I love it because I am so made that I love the beautiful. Thus I love God.' ...

There was another story he told of a king who offered a gift to a rishi. The rishi refused, but the king insisted and begged that he would come with him. When they came to the palace, he heard the king praying, and the king begged for wealth, for power, for length of days from God. The rishi listened, wondering, until at last he picked up his mat and started away. Then the king opened his eyes from his prayers and saw him. 'Why are you going?' he said. 'You have not asked for your gift.' 'I', said the rishi, 'ask from a beggar?' (CW 7:280-281)

27. 'It is also Yours'

I once knew a yogi [Pavhari Baba of Ghazipur], a very old man, who lived in a hole in the ground all by himself. All he had was a pan or two to cook his meals in. He ate very little, and wore scarcely anything, and spent most of his time meditating.

With him all people were alike. He had attained to non-injuring. What he saw in everything, in every person, in every animal, was the Soul, the Lord of the Universe. With him, every person and every animal was 'my Lord'. He never addressed any person or

animal in any other way. Well, one day a thief came his way and stole one of his pans. He saw him and ran after him. The chase was a long one. At last the thief from exhaustion had to stop, and the yogi, running up to him, fell on his knees before him and said, 'My Lord, you do me a great honour to come my way. Do me the honour to accept the other pan. It is also yours.' This old man is dead now. He was full of love for everything in the world. He would have died for an ant. Wild animals instinctively knew this old man to be their friend. Snakes and ferocious animals would go into his hold and sleep with him. They all loved him and never fought in his presence. (CW 6:127)

28. Four Travellers

There were four travellers who came to a high wall. The first one climbed with difficulty to the top and without looking back, jumped over. The second clambered up the wall, looked over, and with a shout of delight disappeared. The third in his turn climbed to the top, looked where his companions had gone, laughed with joy, and followed them. But the fourth one came back to tell what had happened to his fellow-travellers. The sign to us that there is something beyond is the laugh that rings back from those great ones who have plunged from Maya's wall. (CW,7:67)

29. 'I cannot Trade in Love'

One of the disciples of Krishna, the then Emperor of India, was driven from his kingdom by his enemies and had to take shelter with his queen in a forest in the Himalayas, and there one day the queen asked him how it was that he, the most virtuous of men, should suffer so much misery.

Yudhishthira answered, 'Behold, my queen, the Himalayas, how grand and beautiful they are; I love them. They do not give me anything, but my nature is to love the grand, the beautiful, therefore I love them. Similarly, I love the Lord. He is the source of all beauty, of all sublimity. He is the only object to be loved; my nature is to love Him, and therefore I love. I do not pray for anything; I do not ask for anything. Let Him place me wherever He likes. I must love Him for love's sake. I cannot trade love.'(CW, 1:12)

30. Be Pure and Love Everyone

About his [Buddha's] doctrines, some of you know a little. It is his doctrines that appeal to many modern thinkers whom you call agnostics. He was a great preacher of the brotherhood of mankind: 'Aryan or non-Aryan, caste or no caste, and sects or no sects, every one has the same right to God and to religion and to freedom. Come in all of you.' But as to other things, he was very agnostic. 'Be practical.'

There came to him one day five young men, Brahmin born, quarrelling about a question. They came to him to ask him the way to truth. And one said: 'My people teach this, and this is the way to truth.'

The other said: 'I have been taught this, and this is the only way to truth.'

'Which is the right way, sir?'

'Well, you say your people taught this is truth and is the way to God?'

'Yes.'

'But did you see God?'

'No, sir.'

'Your father?'

'No, sir.'

'Your grandfather?'

'No, sir.'

'None of them saw God?'

'No.'

'Well, and your teachers—neither [any] of them saw God?'

'No.'

And he asked the same to the others. They all declared that none had seen God.

'Well,' said Buddha, 'in a certain village came a young man weeping and howling and crying: 'Oh, I love her so! oh my, I love her so!' And then the villagers came; and the only thing he said was he loved her so. 'Who is she that you love?' 'I do not know.' 'Where does she live?' 'I do not know'—but he loved her so. 'How does she look?' 'That I do not know; but oh, I love her so."

Then asked Buddha: 'Young man, what would you call this young man?'

'Why, sir, he was a fool!'

And they all declared: 'Why, sir, that young man was certainly a fool, to be crying and all that about a woman, to say he loved her so much and he never saw her or knew that she existed or anything?'

'Are you not the same? You say that this God your father or your grandfather never saw, and now you are quarrelling upon a thing which neither you nor your ancestors ever knew, and you are trying to cut each other's throats about it.'

Then the young men asked: 'What are we to do?'

'Now, tell me: did your father ever teach that God is ever angry?'

'No, sir.'

'Did your father ever teach that God is evil?'

'No, sir; He is always pure.'

'Well, now, if you are pure and good and all that, do you not think that you will have more chance to come near to that God than by discussing all this and trying to cut each other's throats? Therefore, say I: be pure and be good; be pure and love everyone.' And that was [all]. (CW, 3:525-27)

31. The Highest Love

Next comes Madhura, sweetest love, the love of husband and wife. Of this St. Teresa and the ecstatic saints have been examples. Amongst the Persians, God has been looked upon as the wife, amongst the Hindus as the husband. We may recall the great queen Mira Bai, who preached that the Divine Spouse was all. Some carry this to such an extreme that to call God 'mighty' or 'father' seems to them blasphemy. The language of this worship is erotic. Some even use that of illicit passion. To this cycle belongs the story of Krishna and the Gopi-girls. All this probably seems to you to entail great degeneration on the worshipper. And so it does. Yet many great saints have been developed by it. And no human institution is beyond abuse. Would you cook nothing because there are beggars? Would you possess nothing because there are thieves? 'O Beloved, one kiss of Thy lips, once tasted, hath made me mad!'

The fruit of this idea is that one can no longer belong to any sect, or endure ceremonial. Religion in India culminates in freedom. But even this comes to be given up, and all is love for love's sake.

Last of all comes love without distinction, the Self. There is a Persian poem that tells how a lover came to the door of his beloved, and knocked.

She asked, 'Who art thou?' and he replied, 'I am so and so, thy beloved!' and she answered only, 'Go! I know none such!' But when she had asked for the fourth time, he said, 'I am thyself, O my Beloved, therefore open thou to me!' And the door was opened.

A great saint said, using the language of a girl, describing love: 'Four eyes met. There were changes in two souls. And now I cannot tell whether he is a man and I am a woman, or he is a woman and I a man. This only I remember, two souls were. Love came, and there was one.'

In the highest love, union is only of the spirit. All love of any other kind is quickly evanescent. Only the spiritual lasts, and this grows. (CW, 8:220-21)

32. Nishtha Or Devotion to One Ideal

There is a story of Hanuman, who was a great worshipper of Rama. Just as the Christians worship Christ as the incarnation of God, so the Hindus worship many incarnations of God. According to them, God came nine times in India and will come once more. When he came as Rama, this Hanuman was his great worshipper. Hanuman lived very long and was a great yogi.

During his lifetime, Rama came again as Krishna; and Hanuman, being a great yogi, knew that the same God had come back again as Krishna. He came and served Krishna, but he said to him, 'I want to see that Rama form of yours'. Krishna said, 'Is not this form enough? I am this Krishna;

I am this Rama. All these forms are mine'. Hanuman said,
'I know that, but the Rama form is for me. The Lord of
Janaki [Sita] and the Lord of Sri [Lakshmi or Radha] are
the same. They are both the incarnations of the Supreme
Self. Yet the lotus eyed Rama is my all in all'. This is Ni-
shtha—knowing that all these different forms of worship
are right, yet sticking to one and rejecting the others. We
must not worship the others at all; we must not hate or
criticize them, but respect them. (CW, 9:223-24)

33. The Way of One-pointed Devotion

Many people, in the name of what may be called
religious liberalism, may be seen feeding their
idle curiosity with a continuous succession of
different ideals. With them, hearing new things grows

into a kind of disease, a sort of religious drink-mania. They want to hear new things just by way of getting a temporary nervous excitement, and when one such exciting influence has had its effect on them, they are ready for another. Religion is with these people a sort of intellectual opium-eating, and there it ends.

'There is another sort of man', says Bhagavan Rama-krishna, 'who is like the pearl-oyster of the story. The pearl-oyster leaves its bed at the bottom of the sea, and comes up to the surface to catch the rainwater when the star Svati is in the ascendant. It floats about on the surface of the sea with its shell wide open, until it has succeeded in catching a drop of the rainwater, and then it dives deep down to its sea-bed, and there rests until it has succeed-ed in fashioning as beautiful pearl out of that rain-drop.' (CW, 3:63-64)

34. Courage To Be

There are two sorts of courage. One is the courage of facing the cannon. And the other is the courage of spiritual conviction.

An Emperor who invaded India was told by his teach-er to go and see some of the sages there. After a long search for one, he found a very old man sitting on a block of stone. The Emperor talked with him a little and became very impressed by his wisdom. He asked the sage to go to his country with him.

'No,' said the sage, 'I am quite satisfied with my forest here.'

Said the Emperor, 'I will give you money, position, wealth. I am the Emperor of the world.'

'No,' replied the man.

'I don't care for those things.'

The Emperor replied, 'If you do not go, I will kill you.'

The man smiled serenely and said, 'That is the most foolish thing you have ever said, Emperor. You cannot kill me. Me the sun cannot dry, fire cannot burn, sword cannot kill, for I am the birthless, the deathless, the ever-living omnipotent, omnipresent Spirit.'

This is spiritual boldness, while the other is the courage of a lion or a tiger.

In the Mutiny of 1857 there was a Swami, a very great soul, whom a Mohammedan mutineer stabbed severely. The Hindu mutineers caught and brought the man to the Swami, offering to kill him. But the Swami looked up calmly and said, 'My brother, thou art He, thou art He!' and expired. This is another instance. (CW, 2:84-85)

35. Truth Will Be Out, Sooner Or Later

There was a certain king who had a huge number of courtiers, and each one of these courtiers declared he was ready to sacrifice his life for his master, and that he was the most sincere being ever born. In course of time, a sannyasin came to the king. The king said to him that there never was a king who had so many sincere courtiers as he had. The sannyasin smiled and said he did not believe that. The king said the sannyasin could test it if he liked.

So the sannyasin declared that he would make a great sacrifice by which the king's reign would be extended very long, with the condition that there should be made a small tank into which each one of his courtiers should pour a pitcher of milk, in the dark of night.

The king smiled and said, 'Is this the test?' And he asked his courtiers to come to him, and told them what was to be done. They all expressed their joyful assent to the proposal and returned. In the dead of night, they came and emptied their pitchers into the tank. But in the morning, it was found full of water only. The courtiers were assembled and questioned about the matter. Each one of them had thought there would be so many pitchers of milk that his water would not be detected. Unfortunately most of us have the same idea and we do our share of work as did the courtiers in the story. (CW, 1:427-28)

36. Guru Nanak's Insight

That drill business in the temples and churches— kneeling down at a certain time, standing at ease, and all that drill nonsense, all mechanical, with the

mind thinking of something else—all this has nothing to do with real religion. There was a great prophet in India, Guru Nanak, born [some] four hundred years ago. Some of you have heard of the Sikhs—the fighting people. Guru Nanak was the founder and also a follower of the Sikh religion.

One day he went to the Mohammedans' mosque. These Mohammedans are feared in their own country, just as in a Christian country no one dare say anything against their religion. ... So Guru Nanak went in and there was a big mosque, and the Mohammedans were standing in prayer. They stand in lines: they kneel down, stand up, and repeat certain words at the same times, and one fellow leads. So Guru Nanak went there. And when the mullah was saying 'In the name of the most merciful and kind God, Teacher of all teachers', Guru Nanak began to smile. He says, 'Look at that hypocrite'. The mullah got into a passion. 'Why do you smile?'

'Because you are not praying, my friend. That is why I am smiling.'

'Not praying?'

'Certainly not. There is no prayer in you.'

The mullah was very angry, and he went and laid a complaint before a magistrate and said, 'This heathen rascal dares to come to our mosque and smiles at us when we are praying. The only punishment is instant death. Kill him'.

Guru Nanak was brought before the magistrate and asked why he smiled.

'Because he was not praying.'

'What was he doing?' the magistrate asked.

'I will tell you what he was doing if you will bring him before me.'

The magistrate ordered the mullah to be brought. And when he came, the magistrate said, 'Here is the mullah. [Now] explain why you laughed when he was praying'.

Guru Nanak said, 'Give the mullah a piece of the Koran [to swear on]. [In the mosque] when he was saying 'Allah, Allah', he was thinking of some chicken he had left at home'.

The poor mullah was confounded. He was a little more sincere than the others, and he confessed he was thinking of the chicken, and so they let the Sikh go. 'And', said the magistrate [to the mullah], 'don't go to the mosque again. It is better not to go at all than to commit blasphemy there and hypocrisy. Do not go when you do not feel like praying. Do not be like a hypocrite, and do not think of the chicken and say the name of the Most Merciful and Blissful God'. (CW, 9:232-33)

37. Great Indian Women

Some of you may have heard of the woman [Lakshmi Bai, Queen of Jhansi] who, during the Mutiny of 1857, fought against the English soldiers and held her own ground for two years—leading modern armies, managing batteries and always charging at the head of her army. This queen was a Brahmin girl.

A man whom I know lost three of his sons in that war. When he talks of them he is calm, but when he talks of this woman his voice becomes animated. He used to say that she was a goddess—she was not a human being. This old veteran thinks he never saw better generalship.

The story of Chand Bibi, or Chand Sultana [1546-1599], is well known in India. She was the Queen of Gol-

conda, where the diamond mines were. For months she defended herself. At last, a breach was made in the walls. When the imperial army tried to rush in there, she was in full armour, and she forced the troops to go back. *

*The soldiers were so impressed with Chand Bibi's military prowess and courage that they referred to her as Chand Sultana, which means 'Chand—the Empress'. (CW, 9:200-201)

38. Arise, Awake!

I n New York I used to observe the Irish colonists come—downtrodden, haggard-looking, destitute of all possessions at home, penniless, and wooden-headed—with their only belongings, a stick and a bundle of rags hanging at the end of it, fright in their steps, alarm in their eyes. A different spectacle in six months—the man walks upright, his attire is changed! In his eyes and steps there is no more sign of fright. What is the cause?

Our Vedanta says that that Irishman was kept surrounded by contempt in his own country—the whole of nature was telling him with one voice, 'Pat, you have no more hope, you are born a slave and will remain so.' Having been thus told from his birth, Pat believed in it and hypnotised himself that he was very low, and the Brahman in him shrank away. While no sooner had he landed in America than he heard the shout going up on all sides, 'Pat, you are a man as we are. It is man who has done all, a man like you and me can do everything: have courage!' Pat raised his head and saw that it was so, the Brahman within woke up. Nature herself spoke, as it were, 'Arise, awake, and stop not till the goal is reached.' (CW, 4:483)

39. Thief and a Non-killer

Once a thief broke into the house of a man of this non-killing type. The boys of the house caught hold of the thief and were giving him a sound beating. The master hearing a great row came out on the upper balcony and after making inquiries shouted out, 'Cease from beating, my boys. Don't beat him. Non-injury is the highest virtue.' The fraternity of junior non-killers stopped beating and asked the master what they were to do with the thief.

The master ordered, 'Put him in a bag, and throw him into water.' The thief, much obliged at this humane dispensation, with folded hands said, 'Oh! How great is the master's compassion!' (CW, 7:337)

40. Believe in Yourselves

In the history of each nation, you will always find that only those individuals who have believed in themselves have become great and strong. Here, to India, came an

Englishman who was only a clerk, and for want of funds and other reasons he twice tried to blow his brains out; and when he failed, he believed in himself, he believed that he was born to do great things; and that man became Lord Clive, the founder of the Empire. If he had believed the Padres and gone crawling all his life —'O Lord, I am weak, and I am low'—where would he have been? In a lunatic asylum. You also are made lunatics by these evil teachings. I have seen, all the world over, the bad effects of these weak teachings of humility destroying the human race. Our children are brought up in this way, and is it a wonder that they become semi-lunatics?

This is teaching on the practical side. Believe, therefore, in yourselves, and if you want material wealth, work it out; it will come to you. If you want to be intellectual, work it out on the intellectual plane, and intellectual giants you shall be. And if you want to attain to freedom, work it out on the spiritual plane, and free you shall be and shall enter into Nirvana, the Eternal Bliss. (CW, 3:427)

HAPPINESS

41. Concept of Heaven

I f we had a heaven like that desired by those to whom sense-enjoyment is the very end of existence, then we would not progress. That would be the most terrible curse we could pronounce on the soul. Is this all we can come to? A little weeping and dancing, and then to die like a dog! What a curse you pronounce on the head of humanity when you long for these things! That is what you do when you cry after the joys of this world, for you do not know what true joy is. What philosophy insists on is not to give up joys, but to know what joy really is.

The Norwegian heaven is a tremendous fighting place where they all sit before Odin; they have a wild boar hunt, and then they go to war and slash each other to pieces. But in some way or other, after a few hours of such fighting, the wounds are all healed up, and they go into a hall where the boar has been roasted and have a carousal. And then the wild boar takes form again, ready to be hunted the next day. This is much the same thing as our heaven, not a whit worse, only our ideas may be a little more refined. We want to hunt wild boars, and get to a place where all enjoyments will continue, just as the Norwegian imagines that the wild boar is hunted and eaten every day, and recovers the next day. (CW, 2:166)

42. Solon and Croesus

Do you remember the story of Solon and Croesus? The king said to the great sage that Asia Minor was a very happy place.

And the sage asked him, 'Who is the happiest man? I have not seen anyone very happy.'

'Nonsense,' said Croesus, 'I am the happiest man in the world.'

'Wait, sir, till the end of your life; don't be in a hurry,' replied the sage and went away.

In course of time that king was conquered by the Persians, and they ordered him to be burnt alive. The funeral pyre was prepared and when poor Croesus saw it, he cried aloud 'Solon! Solon!'

On being asked to whom he referred, he told his story, and the Persian emperor was touched, and saved his life. (CW, 1:409)

43. What Joy Really Is

You have all heard of that rich man in Rome who learnt one day that he had only about a million pounds of his property left; he said, 'What shall I do tomorrow?' and forthwith committed suicide. A million pounds was poverty to him. What is joy, and what is sorrow? It is a vanishing quantity, continually vanishing. When I was a child I thought if I could be a cabman, it would be the very acme of happiness for me to drive about. I do not think so now. To what joy will you cling? This is the one point we must all try to understand, and it is one of the last superstitions to leave us. Everyone's idea of pleasure is different. I have seen a man who is not happy unless he swallows a lump of opium every day. He dreams of a heaven where the land is made of opium. That would be a very bad heaven for me.

Again and again in Arabian poetry we read of heaven with beautiful gardens, through which rivers run. I lived much of my life in a country where there is too much water; many villages are flooded and thousands of lives are sacrificed every year. So, my heaven would not have gardens through which rivers flow; I would have a land where very little rain falls.

Our pleasures are always changing. If a young man dreams of heaven, he dreams of a heaven where he will have a beautiful wife. When that same man becomes old he does not want a wife. It is our necessities which make our heaven, and the heaven changes with the change of our necessities. (CW, 2:165-66)

MAYA

AYAM

44. And This Is Maya

We are all like this in the world. A legend tells how once Narada said to Krishna, 'Lord, show me Maya.'

A few days passed away, and Krishna asked Narada to make a trip with him towards a desert, and after walking for several miles, Krishna said, 'Narada, I am thirsty; can you fetch some water for me?'

'I will go at once, sir, and get you water.'

So Narada went. At a little distance there was a village; he entered the village in search of water and knocked at a door, which was opened by a most beautiful young girl. At the sight of her he immediately forgot that his Master was waiting for water, perhaps dying for the want of it. He forgot everything and began to talk with the girl. All that day, he was again at the house, talking to the girl. That talk ripened into love; he asked the father for the daughter, and they were married and lived there and had children.

Thus twelve years passed. His father-in-law died, he inherited his property. He lived, as he seemed to think, a very happy life with his wife and children, his fields and his cattle, and so forth. Then came a flood.

One night the river rose until it overflowed its banks and flooded the whole village. Houses fell, men and animals were swept away and drowned, and everything was floating in the rush of the stream. Narada had to escape.

With one hand he held his wife, and with the other two of his children; another child was on his shoulders, and he was trying to ford this tremendous flood. After a few steps he found the current was too strong, and the child on his shoulders fell and was borne away. A cry of despair came from Narada. In trying to save that child, he lost his grasp upon one of the others, and it also was lost. At last his wife, whom he clasped with all his might, was torn away by the current, and he was thrown on the bank, weeping and wailing in bitter lamentation.

Behind him there came a gentle voice, 'My child, where is the water? You went to fetch a pitcher of water, and I am waiting for you; you have been gone for quite half an hour.'

'Half an hour!' Narada exclaimed.

Twelve whole years had passed through his mind, and all these scenes had happened in half an hour! And this is Maya. (CW, 2:120-21).

45. Our Predicament

There is a Hindu legend that the Lord was once incarnated on earth as a pig. He had a pig mate and in course of time several little pigs were born to Him. He was very happy with His family, living in the mire, squealing with joy, forgetting His divine glory and lordship. The gods became exceedingly concerned and came to the earth to beg Him to give up the pig body and return to heaven. But the Lord would have none of that; He drove them away. He said He was very happy and did not want to be disturbed. Seeing no other course, the gods destroyed the pig body of the Lord. At once He regained His divine majesty and was astonished that He could have found any joy in being a pig.
People behave in the same way. Whenever they hear of the Impersonal God, they say, 'What will become of my individuality?—my individuality will go!'
Next time that thought comes, remember the pig, and then think what an infinite mine of happiness you have, each one of you. How pleased you are with your present condition! But when you realise what you truly are, you will be astonished that you were unwilling to give up your sense-life. What is there in your personality? Is it any better than that pig life? And this you do not want to give up! Lord bless us all! (CW, 8:127-28)

46. Resolving Our Conflicts

The fox is considered very unholy by the Mohammedans and by the Hindus. Also, if a dog touches any bit of food, it has to be thrown out, it cannot be eaten by any man.

In a certain Mohammedan house a fox entered and took a little bit of the food from the table, ate it up, and fled. The man was a poor man, and had prepared a very nice feast for himself, and that feast was made unholy and he could not eat it. So he went to the mullah, a priest, and said, 'This has happened to me; a fox came and took a mouthful out of my meal. What can be done? I had prepared a feast and wanted so much to eat it, and now comes this fox and destroys the whole affair.'

The mullah thought for a minute and then found only one solution and said, 'The only way for you is to get a dog and make him eat a bit out of the same plate, because dogs and foxes are eternally quarreling. The food that was left by the fox will go into your stomach and that left by the dog will go there too, and both will be purified.'

We are very much in the same predicament. This is a hallucination that we are imperfect; and we take up another, that we have to practice to become perfect. Then one will chase the other, as we can use one thorn to extract another and then throw both away. (CW, 3:16-17)

47. Going Round and Round

In some oil mills in India, bullocks are used that go round and round to grind the oil-seed. There is a yoke on the bullock's neck. They have a piece of wood protruding from the yoke, and on that is fastened a wisp of straw. The bullock is blindfolded in such a way that it can only look forward, and so it stretches its neck to get at the straw; and in doing so, it pushes the piece of wood out a little further; and it makes another attempt with the same result, and yet another, and so on. It never catches the straw, but goes round and round in the hope of getting it, and in so doing, grinds out the oil.

In the same way you and I who are born slaves to nature, money and wealth, wives and children, are always
chasing a wisp of straw, a mere chimera, and are going
through an innumerable round of lives without obtaining
what we seek. (CW, 1:408)

48. The Mirage of the World

Once in Western India I was travelling in the desert
country on the coast of the Indian Ocean. For days
and days I used to travel on foot through the desert, but it was to my surprise that I saw every day beautiful
lakes, with trees all around them, and the shadows of the
trees upside down and vibrating there. 'How wonderful it
looks and they call this a desert country!' I said to myself.
Nearly a month I travelled, seeing these wonderful lakes
and trees and plants.

One day I was very thirsty and wanted to have a drink
of water, so I started to go to one of these clear, beautiful lakes, and as I approached, it vanished. And with a
flash it came to my brain, 'This is the mirage about which
I have read all my life,' and with that came also the idea
that throughout the whole of this month, every day, I had
been seeing the mirage and did not know it.

The next morning I began my march. There was again
the lake, but with it came also the idea that it was the mirage
and not a true lake. So is it with this universe. We are all
travelling in this mirage of the world day after day, month
after month, year after year, not knowing that it is a mirage.
One day it will break up, but it will come back again; the
body has to remain under the power of past Karma, and
so the mirage will come back. This world will come back
upon us so long as we are bound by Karma: men, women,

animals, plants, our attachments and duties, all will come
back to us, but not with the same power. Under the influence of the new knowledge the strength of Karma will be
broken, its poison will be lost. It becomes transformed, for
along with it there comes the idea that we know it now,
that the sharp distinction between the reality and the mirage has been known. (CW, 2:281-82)

49. Alice in Wonderland

One dream follows another without connection.
There is no such thing as law or connection in this
world, but we are thinking that there is a great deal
of connection. All of you have probably read *Alice in Wonderland*. It is the most wonderful book for children that
has been written in this century. When I read it, I was
delighted; it was always in my head to write that sort of
book for children. What pleased me most in it was what
you think most incongruous, that there is no connection
there. One idea comes and jumps into another, without
any connection. When you were children, you thought
that the most wonderful connection. So this man brought
back his thoughts of childhood, which were perfectly
connected to him as a child, and composed this book for
children. And all these books which men write, trying to
make children swallow their own ideas as men, are nonsense. We too are grown-up children, that is all.

The world is the same unconnected thing—*Alice in
Wonderland*—with no connection whatever. When we see
things happen a number of times in a certain sequence, we
call it cause and effect, and say that the thing will happen
again. When this dream changes, another dream will seem
quite as connected as this. When we dream, the things we

see all seem to be connected; during the dream we never think they are incongruous; it is only when we wake that we see the want of connection. When we wake from this dream of the world and compare it with the Reality, it will be found all incongruous nonsense, a mass of incongruity passing before us, we do not know whence or whither, but we know it will end; and this is called Maya, and is like masses of fleeting fleecy clouds. (CW, 3:23-24)

50. Two Birds

The whole of the Vedanta Philosophy is in this story: Two birds of golden plumage sat on the same tree. The one above, serene, majestic, immersed in his own glory; the one below restless and eating the fruits of

the tree, now sweet, now bitter. Once he ate an excep-
tionally bitter fruit, then he paused and looked up at the
majestic bird above; but he soon forgot about the other
bird and went on eating the fruits of the tree as before.
Again he ate a bitter fruit, and this time he hopped up a
few boughs nearer to the bird at the top.

This happened many times until at last the lower bird
came to the place of the upper bird and lost himself. He
found all at once that there had never been two birds, but
that he was all the time that upper bird, serene, majestic,
and immersed in his own glory. (CW, 7:80)

51. 'I am Discovered'

Once a Brahmin, desirous of going to a disciple's
house, was in need of a coolie to carry his load. Not
finding anyone belonging to a good caste, he at last
asked a shoemaker to perform the function. The man at
first refused on the ground, that he was a man belonging
to an untouchable caste. But the Brahmin insisted on en-
gaging him, telling him that he would escape detection by
keeping perfectly silent.

The man was at last persuaded to go, and when the
party reached their destination, someone asked the shoe-
maker-servant to remove a pair of shoes. The servant who
thought it best to keep silent, as instructed, paid no attention to the order, which was repeated, whereupon the
man getting annoyed shouted out, 'Why dost thou not
hear me, sirrah? Art thou a shoemaker?'

'O Master,' cried the bewildered shoemaker, 'I am
discovered. I cannot stay any longer.'

Saying this he immediately took to his heels. (CW,
7:165)

MIND AND CONCENTRATION

52. Intensity of Prayer

Acertain Mohammedan was praying in a garden. They are very regular in their prayers. When the time comes, wherever they are, they just begin, fall down on the ground and get up and fall down, and so on. One of them was in a garden when the call for prayer came, so he knelt there prostrate on the ground to pray. A girl was waiting in the garden for her lover, and she saw him on the other side. And in her hurry to reach him, she did not see the man prostrate and walked over him. He was a fanatical Mohammedan—just what you call here a Presbyterian, the same breed. Both believe in barbecuing eternally. So you can just imagine the anger of this Mohammedan when his body was walked over—he wanted to kill the girl. The girl was a smart one, and she said, 'Stop that nonsense. You are a fool and a hypocrite'.

'What! I am a hypocrite?'

'Yes, I am going to meet my earthly lover, and I did not see you there. But you are going to meet your heavenly lover and should not know that a girl was passing over your body.' (CW, 9:233-34)

53. All Power is within

I shall tell you a story which I heard from a great scholar in the West. It was told him by a Governor of Ceylon who saw the performance. A girl was brought forward and

93

seated cross-legged upon a stool made of sticks crossed. After she had been seated for a time, the show-man began to take out, one after another, these cross-bars; and when all were taken out, the girl was left floating in the air. The Governor thought there was some trick, so he drew his sword and violently passed it under the girl; nothing was there.

Now, what was this? It was not magic or something extraordinary. That is the peculiarity. No one in India would tell you that things like this do not exist. To the Hindu it is a matter of course. You know what the Hindus would often say when they have to

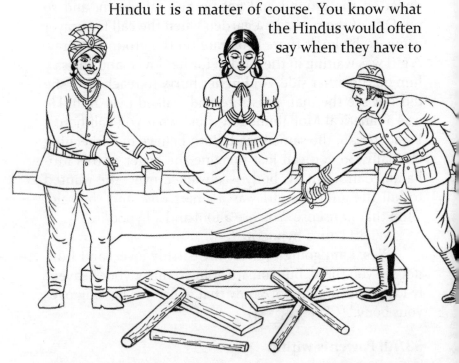

fight their enemies—'Oh, one of our yogis will come and drive the whole lot out!' It is the extreme belief of the race. What power is there in the hand or the sword? The power is all in the spirit. (CW, 2:21)

54. The Tartar Inside

You know the story of the man who caught a Tartar. A soldier was outside the town, and he cried out when he came near the barracks, 'I have caught a Tartar.'
A voice called out, 'Bring him in.'
'He won't come in, sir.'
'Then you come in.'
'He won't let me come in, sir.'
So, in this mind of ours, we have 'caught a Tartar': neither can we tone it down, nor will it let us be toned down. We have all 'caught Tartars'. We all say, be quiet, and peaceful, and so forth. But every baby can say that and thinks he can do it. However, that is very difficult. I have tried. I threw overboard all my duties and fled to the tops of mountains; I lived in caves and deep forests—but all the same, I 'caught a Tartar', because I had my world with me all the time. The 'Tartar' is what I have in my own mind, so we must not blame poor people outside. 'These circumstances are good, and these are bad,' so we say, while the 'Tartar' is here, within; if we can quiet him down, we shall be all right. (CW, 4:130, 131)

55. The Noseless Saint

The present writer [Swamiji] had occasion to ask the saint [Pavahari Baba] the reason for his not coming out of his cave to help the world. At first, with his native humility and humour, he gave the following strong reply:
'A certain wicked person was caught in some criminal act and had his nose cut off as a punishment. Ashamed

to show his noseless features to the world and disgusted with himself, he fled into a forest; and there, spreading a tiger-skin on the ground, he would feign deep meditation whenever he thought anybody was about. This conduct, instead of keeping people off, drew them in crowds to pay their respects to this wonderful saint; and he found that his forest-life had brought him once again an easy living.

Thus years went by. At last the people around became very eager to listen to some instruction from the lips

of the silent meditative saint; and one young man was specially anxious to be initiated into the order. It came to such a pass that any more delay in that line would undermine the reputation of the saint. So one day he broke his silence and asked the enthusiastic young man to bring on the morrow a sharp razor with him. The young man, glad at the prospect of the great desire of his life being speedily fulfilled, came early the next morning with the razor. The noseless saint led him to a very retired spot in the forest, took the razor in his hand, opened it, and with one stroke cut off his nose, repeating in a solemn voice, 'Young man, this has been my initiation into the order. The same I give to you. Do you transmit it diligently to others when the opportunity comes!' The young man could not divulge the secret of this wonderful initiation for shame, and carried out to the best of his ability the injunctions of his master. Thus a whole sect of nose-cut saints spread over the country. Do you want me to be the founder of another such?'

Later on, in a more serious mood, another query brought the answer: 'Do you think that physical help is the only help possible? Is it not possible that one mind can help other minds even without the activity of the body?' (CW, 4:292)

56. All Powers are in the Mind

All over the world there has been the belief in the supernatural throughout the ages. All of us have heard of extraordinary happenings, and many of us have had some personal experience of them. I would rather introduce the subject by telling you certain facts which have come within my own experience. I once heard of a man who, if any one went to him with questions in his mind, would answer them immediately; and I was also informed that he foretold events. I was curious and went to see him with a few friends. We each had something in our minds to ask, and, to avoid mistakes, we wrote down our questions and put them in our pockets. As soon as the man saw one of us, he repeated our questions and gave the answers to them. Then he wrote something on paper, which he folded up, asked me to sign on the back, and said, 'Don't look at it; put it in your pocket and keep it there till I ask for it again.' And so on to each one of us.

He next told us about some events that would happen to us in the future. Then he said, 'Now, think of a word or a sentence, from any language you like.'

I thought of a long sentence from Sanskrit, a language of which he was entirely ignorant. 'Now, take out the paper from your pocket,' he said. The Sanskrit sentence was written there! He had written it an hour before with the remark, 'In confirmation of what I have written, this man will think of this sentence.' It was correct.

Another of us who had been given a similar paper which he had signed and placed in his pocket, was also asked to think of a sentence. He thought of a sentence in Arabic, which it was still less possible for the man to know; it was some passage from the Koran. And my friend found this written down on the paper.

Another of us was a physician. He thought of a sentence from a German medical book. It was written on his paper.

Several days later I went to this man again, thinking possibly I had been deluded somehow before. I took other friends, and on this occasion also he came out wonderfully triumphant.

Another time I was in the city of Hyderabad in India, and I was told of a Brahmin there who could produce numbers of things from where, nobody knew. This man was in business there; he was a respectable gentleman. And I asked him to show me his tricks. It so happened that this man had a fever, and in India there is a general belief that if a holy man puts his hand on a sick man he would be well. This Brahmin came to me and said, 'Sir, put your hand on my head, so that my fever may be cured.' I said, 'Very good; but you show me your tricks.' He promised. I put my hand on his head as desired, and later he came to fulfil his promise.

He had only a strip of cloth about his loins, we took off everything else from him. I had a blanket which I gave him to wrap round himself, because it was cold, and made him sit in a corner. Twenty-five pairs of eyes were looking at him. And he said, 'Now, look, write down anything you want.' We all wrote down names of fruits that never grew in that country, bunches of grapes, oranges, and so on. And we gave him those bits of paper. And there came from under his blanket, bushels of grapes, oranges, and so forth, so much that if all that fruit was weighed, it would have been twice as heavy as the man. He asked us to eat the fruit. Some of us objected, thinking it was hypnotism; but the man began eating himself—so we all ate. It was all right. He ended by producing a mass of roses. Each flower was perfect, with dew-drops on the petals, not one crushed, not one injured. And masses of them! When I asked the man for an explanation, he said, 'It is all sleight of hand.'

Whatever it was, it seemed to be impossible that it could be sleight of hand merely. From whence could he have got such large quantities of things?

Well, I saw many things like that. Going about India you find hundreds of similar things in different places. These are in every country. Even in this country you will find some such wonderful things. Of course there is a great deal of fraud, no doubt; but then, whenever you see fraud, you have also to say that fraud is an imitation.

There must be some truth somewhere, that is being imitated; you cannot imitate nothing. Imitation must be of something substantially true.

In very remote times in India, thousands of years ago, these facts used to happen even more than they do today. It seems to me that when a country becomes very thickly populated, psychical power deteriorates. Given a vast country thinly inhabited, there will, perhaps, be more of psychical power there. These facts, the Hindus, being analytically minded, took up and investigated. And they came to certain conclusions; that is, they made a science of it. They found out that all these, though extraordinary, are also natural; there is nothing supernatural. They are under laws just the same as any other physical phenomenon. It is not a freak of nature that a man is born with such powers. They can be systematically studied, practised, and acquired. This science they call the science of Raja-yoga. There are thousands of people who cultivate the study of this science, and for the whole nation it has become a part of daily worship.

The conclusion they have reached is that all these extraordinary powers are in the mind of man. (CW, 2: 10-12)

57. Be Like a Pearl Oyster

There is a pretty Indian fable to the effect that if it rains when the star Svati is in the ascendant, and a drop of rain falls into an oyster, that drop becomes a pearl. The oysters know this, so they come to the surface when that star shines, and wait to catch the precious raindrop. When a drop falls into them, quickly the oysters close their shells and dive down to the bottom of the sea, there to patiently develop the drop into the pearl. We should be like that. First hear, then understand, and then, leaving all distractions, shut your minds to outside influences, and devote yourselves to developing the truth within you. There is the danger of frittering away your energies by taking up an idea only for its novelty, and then giving it up for another that is newer.

Take one thing up and do it, and see the end of it, and before you have seen the end, do not give it up. He who can become mad with an idea, he alone sees light. Those that only take a nibble here and a nibble there will never attain anything. They may titillate their nerves for a moment, but there it will end. They will be slaves in the hands of nature, and will never get beyond the senses. (CW, 1: 177)

FAITH AND SACRIFICE

58. Pratika Or Symbolism

There was a certain yogi who used to practise meditation in a lonely part of the forest, on the banks of a river. There was a poor cowherd, a very ignorant man, who used to tend his herd in that forest. Every day he used to see this same yogi meditating by the hour, practising austerities, living alone and studying. Somehow the cowherd got curious as to what he did. So he came to the yogi and said, 'Sir, can you teach me the way to God?' This yogi was a very learned, great man, and he replied, 'How will you understand God—you common cowherd? Blockhead, go home and tend your cows and don't bother your head with such things.'

The poor fellow went away, but somehow a real want had come to him. So he could not rest, and he came again to the yogi and said, 'Sir, won't you teach me something about God?'

Again he was repulsed: 'Oh, you blockhead, what can you understand of God? Go home.' But the cowherd could not sleep; he could not eat. He must know something about God.

So he came again; and the yogi, in order to quiet the man, as he was so insisting, said, 'I'll teach you about God.'

The man asked, 'Sir, what sort of being is God? What is His form? How does He look?'

The yogi said, 'God is just like the big bull in your herd. That is just God. God has become that big bull.'

The man believed him and went back to his herd. Day and night he took that bull for God and began to worship it. He brought the greenest grass for that bull, rested close to it and gave it light, sat near it and followed it. Thus days and months and years passed. His whole soul was there [in the bull].

One day he heard a voice, as it were, coming out of the bull. 'The bull speaks!' [the cowherd thought.]

'My son, my son.'

'Why, the bull is speaking! No, the bull cannot speak.'

Again the voice came, and that time he found it out. It was from his own heart. He found that God was in him. Then he learned the wonderful truth of the Teacher of all teachers: 'I am with thee always.' And the poor cowherd learned the whole mystery.

Then he goes back to the yogi, and when he is at some distance the yogi sees him. The yogi has been the most learned man in the country, practising austerity for years—meditating, studying. And this cowherd, an ignorant blockhead, never studied a book nor learned his letters. But he comes—his whole body, as it were, transfigured, his face changed, the light of heaven shining round his face. The yogi got up. 'What is this change? Where did you get this?'

'Sir, you gave me that.'

'How? I told you that in joke.'

'But I took it seriously. And I got everything I wanted out of that bull, for is He not everywhere?'

So that bull was the Pratika. And that man worshipped the bull as his Pratika—as God—and he got everything out of it. So that intense love—that desire—brings out everything. Everything is in ourselves, and the external world and the external worship are the forms, the suggestions that call it out. When they become strong, the Lord within awakens. (CW. 9:229-30)

59. A Case of Complete Self-sacrifice

This idea of complete self-sacrifice is illustrated in the following story: After the battle of Kurukshetra the five Pandava brothers performed a great sacrifice and made very large gifts to the poor. All people expressed amazement at the greatness and richness of the sacrifice, and said that such a sacrifice the world had never seen before.

But, after the ceremony, there came a little mongoose, half of whose body was golden, and the other half brown; and he began to roll on the floor of the sacrificial hall. He said to those around, 'You are all liars; this is no sacrifice.'

'What!' they exclaimed, 'you say this is no sacrifice; do you not know how money and jewels were poured out to the poor and every one became rich and happy? This was the most wonderful sacrifice any man every performed.'

But the mongoose said, 'There was once a little village, and in it there dwelt a poor Brahmin with his wife, his son, and his son's wife. They were very poor and lived on small gifts made to them for preaching and teaching. There came in that land a three years' famine, and the poor Brahmin suffered more than ever. At last when the family had starved for days, the father brought home one morning a little barley flour, which he had been fortunate enough to obtain, and he divided it into four parts, one for each member of the family. They prepared it for their meal, and just as they were about to eat, there was a knock at the door. The father opened it, and there stood a guest. Now in India a guest is a sacred person; he is as a god for the time being, and must be treated as such.

So the poor Brahmin said, 'Come in, sir; you are welcome.' He set before the guest his own portion of the food, which the guest quickly ate and said, 'Oh, sir, you have killed me; I have been starving for ten days, and this little bit has but increased my hunger.'

Then the wife said to her husband, 'Give him my share,' but the husband said, 'Not so.'

The wife however insisted, saying, 'Here is a poor man, and it is our duty as householders to see that he is fed, and it is my duty as a wife to give him my portion, seeing that you have no more to offer him.'

Then she gave her share to the guest, which he ate, and said he was still burning with hunger. So the son said, 'Take my portion also; it is the duty of a son to help his father to fulfil his obligation.'

The guest ate that, but remained still unsatisfied; so the son's wife gave him her portion also. That was sufficient, and the guest departed, blessing them.

That night those four people died of starvation. A few granules of that flour had fallen on the floor; and when I rolled my body on them, half of it became golden, as you see. Since then I have been travelling all over the world, hoping to find another sacrifice like that, but nowhere have I found one; nowhere else has the other half of my body been turned into gold. That is why I say this is no sacrifice.'

This idea of charity is going out of India; great men are becoming fewer and fewer. When I was first learning English, I read an English story book in which there was a story about a dutiful boy who had gone out to work and had given some of his money to his old mother, and this was praised in three or four pages. What was that? No Hindu boy can ever understand the moral of that story. Now I understand it when I hear the Western idea—every man for himself. And some men take everything for themselves, and fathers and mothers and wives and children go to the wall. That should never and nowhere be the ideal of the householder. (CW, 1:60-62)

60. The Bell-Eared Demon (ghanta karna)

Take up one idea, your Ishta, and let the whole soul be devoted to it. Practise this from day to day until you see the result, until the soul grows. And if it is sincere and good, that very idea will spread till it covers the whole universe. Let it spread by itself; it will all come from the inside out. Then you will say that your Ishta is everywhere and that He is in everything.

Of course, at the same time, we must always remem-

ber that we must recognize the Ishtas of others and respect them—the other ideas of God—or else worship
will degenerate into fanaticism. There is an old story of
a man who was a worshipper of Shiva. There are sects in
our country who worship God as Shiva, and others who
worship Him as Vishnu. This man was a great worshipper
of Shiva, and to that he added a tremendous hatred for
all worshippers of Vishnu and would not hear the name
of Vishnu pronounced. There are a great number of worshippers of Vishnu in India, and he could not avoid hearing the name. So he bored two holes in his ears and tied
two little bells onto them. Whenever a man mentioned
the name of Vishnu, he moved his head and rang the bells,
and that prevented his hearing the name.

But Shiva told him in a dream, 'What a fool you are! I
am Vishnu, and I am Shiva; they are not different—only in
name. There are not two Gods.' But this man said, 'I don't
care. I will have nothing to do with this Vishnu business.'

He had a little statue of Shiva and made it very nice,
built an altar for it. One day he bought some beautiful incense and went home to light some of the incense for his
God. While the fumes [smoke] of his incense were rising in
the air, he found that the image was divided into two: one
half remained Shiva, and the other half was Vishnu. Then
the man jumped up and put his finger under the nostril of
Vishnu so that not a particle of the smell could get there.

Then Shiva became disgusted, and the man became
[was turned into] a demon. He is [known as] the father of
all fanatics, the 'bell eared' demon. He is respected by the
boys of India, and they worship him. It is a very peculiar
kind of worship. They make a clay image and worship him
with all sorts of horrible smelling flowers. There are some
flowers in the forests of India which have a most pestilen-

tial smell. They worship him with these and then take big sticks and beat the image. He [the 'bell eared' demon] is the father of all fanatics who hate all other gods except their own. (CW, 9:225-26)

61. Each is Great in His Own Place

A certain king used to inquire of all the sannyasins that came to his country, 'Which is the greater man—he who gives up the world and becomes a sannyasin, or he who lives in the world and performs his duties as a householder?' Many wise men sought to solve the problem. Some asserted that the sannyasin was the greater, upon which the king demanded that they should prove their assertion. When they could not, he ordered them to marry and become householders. Then others came and said, 'The householder who performs his duties is the greater man.' Of them, too the king demanded proofs. When they could not give them, he made them also settle down as householders.

At last there came a young sannyasin, and the king similarly inquired of him also.

He answered, 'Each, O king, is equally great in his place.'

'Prove this to me,' asked the king.

'I will prove it to you,' said the sannyasin, 'but you must first come and live as I do for a few days, that I may be able to prove to you what I say.'

The king consented and followed the sannyasin out of his own territory and passed through many other countries until they came to a great kingdom. In the capital of that kingdom a great ceremony was going on. The king and the sannyasin heard the noise of drums and music, and heard also the criers; the people were assembled in the streets in gala dress, and a great proclamation was being made. The king and the sannyasin stood there to see what was going on. The crier was proclaiming loudly that the princess, daughter of the king of that country, was about to choose a husband from among those assembled before her.

It was an old custom in India for princesses to choose husbands in this way. Each princess had certain ideas of the sort of man she wanted for a husband. Some would have the handsomest man, others would have only the most learned, others again the richest, and so on. All the princes of the neighbourhood put on their bravest attire and presented themselves before her. Sometimes they too had their own criers to enumerate their advantages and the reasons why they hoped the princess would choose them. The princess was taken round on a throne, in the most splendid array, and looked at and heard about them. If she was not pleased with what she saw and heard, she said to her bearers, 'Move on,' and no more notice was taken of the rejected suitors. If, however, the princess was pleased with any one of them, she threw a garland of flowers over him and he became her husband.

The princess of the country to which our king and the sannyasin had come was having one of these interesting ceremonies. She was the most beautiful princess in the world, and the husband of the princess would be ruler of the kingdom after her father's death. The idea of this princess was to marry the handsomest man, but she could not find the right one to please her. Several times these meetings had taken place, but the princess could not select a husband. This meeting was the most splendid of all; more people than ever had come to it. The princess came in on a throne, and the bearers carried her from place to place. She did not seem to care for any one, and every one became disappointed that this meeting also was going to be a failure.

Just then came a young man, a sannyasin, handsome as if the sun had come down to the earth, and stood in one corner of the assembly, watching what was going on. The throne with the princess came near him, and as soon as she saw the beautiful sannyasin, she stopped and threw the garland over him. The young sannyasin seized the garland and threw it off, exclaiming, 'What nonsense is this? I am a sannyasin. What is marriage to me?'

The king of that country thought that perhaps this man was poor and so dared not marry the princess, and said to him, 'With my daughter goes half my kingdom now, and the whole kingdom after my death!' and put the garland again on the sannyasin.

The young man threw it off once more, saying, 'Nonsense! I do not want to marry,' and walked quickly away from the assembly.

Now the princess had fallen so much in love with this young man that she said, 'I must marry this man or I shall die'; and she went after him to bring him back.

Then our other sannyasin, who had brought the king

there, said to him, 'King, let us follow this pair'; so they walked after them, but at a good distance behind.

The young sannyasin who had refused to marry the princess walked out into the country for several miles. When he came to a forest and entered into it, the princess followed him, and the other two followed them. Now this young sannyasin was well acquainted with that forest and knew all the intricate paths in it. He suddenly passed into one of these and disappeared, and the princess could not discover him. After trying for a long time to find him she sat down under a tree and began to weep, for she did not know the way out. Then our king and the other sannyasin came up to her and said, 'Do not weep; we will show you the way out of this forest, but it is too dark for us to find it now. Here is a big tree; let us rest under it, and in the morning we will go early and show you the road.'

Now a little bird and his wife and their three little ones lived on that tree, in a nest. This little bird looked down and saw the three people under the tree and said to his wife, 'My dear, what shall we do? Here are some guests in the house, and it is winter, and we have no fire.'

So he flew away and got a bit of burning firewood in his beak and dropped it before the guests, to which they added fuel and made a blazing fire. But the little bird was not satisfied.

He said again to his wife, 'My dear, what shall we do? There is nothing to give these people to eat, and they are hungry. We are householders; it is our duty to feed any one who comes to the house. I must do what I can, I will give them my body.'

So he plunged into the midst of the fire and perished. The guests saw him falling and tried to save him, but he was too quick for them.

The little bird's wife saw what her husband did, and she said, 'Here are three persons and only one little bird for them to eat. It is not enough; it is my duty as a wife not to let my husband's effort go in vain; let them have my body also.' Then she fell into the fire and was burned to death.

Then the three baby-birds, when they saw what was done and that there was still not enough food for the three guests, said, 'Our parents have done what they could and still it is not enough. It is our duty to carry on the work of our parents; let our bodies go too.' And they all dashed down into the fire also.

Amazed at what they saw, the three people could not of course eat these birds. They passed the night without food, and in the morning the king and the sannyasin showed the princess the way, and she went back to her father.

Then the sannyasin said to the king, 'King, you have seen that each is great in his own place. If you want to live in the world, live like those birds, ready at any moment to sacrifice yourself for others. If you want to renounce the world, be like that young man to whom the most beautiful woman and a kingdom were as nothing. If you want to be a householder, hold your life a sacrifice for the welfare of others; and if you choose the life of renunciation, do not even look at beauty and money and power. Each is great in his own place, but the duty of the one is not the duty of the other.' (CW, 1:47-51)

62. Shraddha or Genuine Faith

We must always remember that our backbone is spirituality, and to do that we must have a guide who will show the path to us, that path about which I am talking just now. If any of you do not believe it, if there be a Hindu boy amongst us who is not ready to believe that his religion is pure spirituality, I do not call him a Hindu.

I remember in one of the villages of Kashmir, while talking to an old Mohammedan lady, I asked her in a mild voice, 'What religion is yours?'

She replied in her own language, 'Praise the Lord! By the mercy of God, I am a Mussalman.'

And then I asked a Hindu, 'What is your religion?' He plainly replied, 'I am a Hindu.'

I remember that grand word of the Katha Upanishad—*shraddha* or marvellous faith. An instance of Shraddha can be found in the life of Nachiketa. To preach the doctrine of Shraddha or genuine faith is the mission of my life. Let me repeat to you that this faith is one of the potent factors of humanity and of all religions. First, have faith in yourselves. Know that though one may be a little bubble and another may be a mountain-high wave, yet behind both the bubble and the wave there is the infinite ocean.
(CW, 3:444)

WOMEN OF INDIA

63. Sita-Rama, the Ideal Couple

Rama is considered the type of the Absolute, and Sita that of Power. We have no time to go over all the life of Sita, but I will quote a passage from her life that is very much suited to the ladies of this country.

The picture opens when she was in the forest with her husband, whither they were banished. There was a female sage whom they both went to see. Her fasts and devotions had emaciated her body.

Sita approached this sage and bowed down before her. The sage placed her hand on the head of Sita and said: 'It is a great blessing to possess a beautiful body; you have that. It is a greater blessing to have a noble husband; you have that. It is the greatest blessing to be perfectly obedient to such a husband; you are that. You must be happy.'

Sita replied, 'Mother, I am glad that God has given me a beautiful body and that I have so devoted a husband. But as to the third blessing, I do not know whether I obey him or he obeys me. One thing alone I remember, that when he took me by the hand before the sacrificial fire—whether it was a reflection of the fire or whether God himself made it appear to me—I found that I was his and he was mine. And since then, I have found that I am the complement of his life, and he of mine.'

Portions of this poem have been translated into the English language. Sita is the ideal of a woman in India and worshipped as God incarnate. (CW, 9:195-96)

64. A Heroic Act

A Rajput prince of Kanauj—a very ancient city—had a daughter [Samyukta]. She had heard of the military fame of Prithvi Rai [King of Ajmere and Delhi] and all his glory, and she was in love with him. Now her father wanted to hold a Rajasuya sacrifice, so he invited all the kings in the country. And in that sacrifice, they all had to render menial service to him because he was superior over all; and with that sacrifice he declared there would be a choice by his daughter.

But the daughter was already in love with Prithvi Rai. He was very mighty and was not going to acknowledge loyalty to the king, her father, so he refused the invitation. Then the king made a golden statue of Prithvi Rai and put it near the door. He said that that was the duty he had given him to perform—that of a porter.

The upshot of the whole affair was that Prithvi Rai, like a true knight, came and took the lady behind him on his horse, and they both fled.

When the news came to her father, he gave chase with his army, and there was a great battle in which the majority of both armies was killed. And [thus the Rajputs were so weakened that] the Mohammedan empire in India began.

When the Mohammedan empire was being established in northern India, the Queen of Chitore [Rani Padmini] was famed for her beauty. And the report of her beauty reached the sultan, and he wrote a letter for the queen to be sent to his harem. The result was a terrible war between the King of Chitore and the sultan. The Mohammedans invaded Chitore. And when the Rajputs found they could not defend themselves any more, the men all took sword in hand and killed and were killed, and the women perished in the flames.

After the men had all perished, the conqueror entered the city. There in the street was rising a horrible flame. He saw circles of women going around it, led by the queen herself. When he approached near and asked the queen to refrain from jumping into the flames, she said, 'This is how the Rajput woman treats you', and threw herself into the fire.

It is said that 74,500 women perished in the flames that day to save their honour from the hands of the Mohammedans. Even today when we write a letter, after sealing it we write '74½' upon it, meaning that if one dares to open this letter, that sin of killing 74,500 women will be upon his head. (CW, 9:198-99)

65.   Raksha Bandhan

I will tell you the story of another beautiful Rajput girl.* There is a peculiar custom in our country called 'protection'. Women can send small bracelets of silken thread to men. And if a girl sends one of these to a man, that man becomes her brother.

During the reign of the last of the Mogul emperors—the cruel man who destroyed that most brilliant empire of India—he similarly heard of the beauty of a Rajput chieftain's daughter. Orders were sent that she should be brought to the Mogul harem.

Then a messenger came from the emperor to her with his picture, and he showed it to her. In derision she stamped upon it with her feet and said, 'Thus the Rajput girl treats your Mogul emperor.' As a result, the imperial army was marched into Rajputana.

In despair the chieftain's daughter thought of a device. She took a number of these bracelets and sent them to the Rajput princes with a message: 'Come and help us.' All the Rajputs assembled, and so the imperial forces had to go back again. (CW, 9:199-200)

66. The Status of Women in the Vedas

Do you remember how Yajnavalkya was questioned at the Court of King Janaka? His principal examiner was Vachaknavi, the maiden orator—brahmavadini, as the word of the day was. 'Like two shining arrows in the hand of the skilled archer', she says, 'are my questions.' Her sex is not even commented upon.

Again, could anything be more complete than the equality of boys and girls in our old forest universities? Read our Sanskrit dramas—read the story of Shakuntala, and see if Tennyson's 'Princess' has anything to teach us!'(CW, 5:230)

ATTITUDE

67. Be Active First

I once met a man in my country whom I had known before as a very stupid, dull person, who knew nothing and had not the desire to know anything, and was living the life of a brute.

He asked me what he should do to know God, how he was to get free.

'Can you tell a lie?' I asked him.

'No,' he replied.

'Then you must learn to do so. It is better to tell a lie than to be a brute, or a log of wood. You are inactive; you have not certainly reached the highest state, which is beyond all actions, calm and serene; you are too dull even to do something wicked.'

That was an extreme case, of course, and I was joking with him; but what I meant was that a man must be active in order to pass through activity to perfect calmness. (CW, 1:39-40)

68. We, Not the World, Get Straightened Out

There was a poor man who wanted some money; and somehow he had heard that if he could get hold of a ghost, he might command him to bring money or anything else he liked; so he was very anxious to get hold of a ghost. He went about searching for a man who would give him a ghost, and at last he found a sage with great

powers, and besought his help.

The sage asked him what he would do with a ghost. 'I want a ghost to work for me; teach me how to get hold of one, sir; I desire it very much,' replied the man.

But the sage said, 'Don't disturb yourself, go home.'

The next day the man went again to the sage and began to weep and pray, 'Give me a ghost; I must have a ghost, sir, to help me.'

At last the sage was disgusted, and said, 'Take this charm, repeat this magic word, and a ghost will come, and whatever you say to him he will do. But beware; they are terrible beings, and must be kept continually busy. If you fail to give him work, he will take your life.'

The man replied, 'That is easy; I can give him work for all his life.'

Then he went to a forest, and after long repetition of the magic word, a huge ghost appeared before him, and said, 'I am a ghost. I have been conquered by your magic; but you must keep me constantly employed. The moment you fail to give me work I will kill you.'

The man said, 'Build me a palace,' and the ghost said, 'It is done; the palace is built.'

'Bring me money,' said the man.

'Here is your money,' said the ghost.

'Cut this forest down, and build a city in its place.'

'That is done,' said the ghost, 'anything more?'

Now the man began to be frightened and thought he could give him nothing more to do; he did everything in a trice.

The ghost said, 'Give me something to do or I will eat you up.' The poor man could find no further occupation for him, and was frightened. So he ran and ran and at last reached the sage, and said, 'Oh, sir, protect my life!'

The sage asked him what the matter was, and the man replied, 'I have nothing to give the ghost to do. Everything I tell him to do he does in a moment, and he threatens to eat me up if I do not give him work.'

Just then the ghost arrived, saying, 'I'll eat you up,' and he would have swallowed the man. The man began to shake, and begged the sage to save his life.

The sage said, 'I will find you a way out. Look at that dog with a curly tail. Draw your sword quickly and cut the tail off and give it to the ghost to straighten out.'

The man cut off the dog's tail and gave it to the ghost, saying, 'Straighten that out for me.'

The ghost took it and slowly and carefully straightened it out, but as soon as he let it go, it instantly curled up again. Once more he laboriously straightened it out, only to find it again curled up as soon as he attempted to let go of it. Again he patiently straightened it out, but as soon as he let it go, it curled up

again. So he went on for days and days, until he was exhausted and said, 'I was never in such trouble before in my life. I am an old veteran ghost, but never before was I in such trouble.'

'I will make a compromise with you,' he said to the man, 'you let me off and I will let you keep all I have given you and will promise not to harm you.'

The man was much pleased, and accepted the offer gladly.

This world is like a dog's curly tail, and people have been striving to straighten it out for hundreds of years; but when they let it go, it has curled up again. How could it be otherwise? One must first know how to work without attachment, then one will not be a fanatic. When we know that this world is like a dog's curly tail and will never get straightened, we shall not become fanatics. (CW, 1:77-79)

69. Narada and Two Aspirants

There was a great god-sage called Narada. Just as there are sages among mankind, great yogis, so there are great yogis among the gods. Narada was a good yogi, and very great. He travelled everywhere. One day he was passing through a forest, and saw a man who had been meditating until the white ants had built a huge mound round his body— so long had he been sitting in that position.

He said to Narada, 'Where are you going?'

Narada replied, 'I am going to heaven.'

'Then ask God when He will be merciful to me; when I shall attain freedom.'

Further on Narada saw another man. He was jumping about, singing, dancing, and said, 'Oh, Narada, where are you going?' His voice and his gestures were wild. Narada said, 'I am going to heaven.'

'Then, ask when I shall be free.'

Narada went on. In the course of time he came again by the same road, and there was the man who had been meditating with the ant-hill round him. He said, 'Oh, Narada, did you ask the Lord about me?'

'Oh, yes.'

'What did He say?'

'The Lord told me that you would attain freedom in four more births.'

Then the man began to weep and wail, and said, 'I have meditated until an ant-hill has grown around me, and I have four more births yet!'

Narada went to the other man. 'Did you ask my question?' 'Oh, yes. Do you see this tamarind tree? I have to tell you that as many leaves as there are on that tree, so many times, you shall be born, and then you shall attain freedom.'

The man began to dance for joy, and said, 'I shall have freedom after such a short time!'

A voice came, 'My child, you will have freedom this minute.' That was the reward for his perseverance. He was ready to work through all those births, nothing discouraged him. But the first man felt that even four more births were too long. Only perseverance, like that of the man who was willing to wait aeons brings about the highest result. (CW, 1:193-94)

70. Universal Brotherhood

I remember an old story. In India, taking wine is considered very bad. There were two brothers who wished, one night, to drink wine secretly; and their uncle, who was a very orthodox man, was sleeping in a room quite close to theirs.

So, before they began to drink, they said to each other, 'We must be very silent, or uncle will wake up.'

When they were drinking, they continued repeating to each other 'Silence! Uncle will wake up', each trying to shout the other down. And, as the shouting increased, the uncle woke up, came into the room, and discovered the whole thing.

Now, we all shout like these drunken men, 'Universal brotherhood! We are all equal, therefore let us make a sect.' As soon as you make a sect you protest against equality, and equality is no more. Mohammedans talk of universal brotherhood, but what comes out of that in reality? Why, anybody who is not a Mohammedan will not be admitted into the brotherhood; he will more likely have his throat cut. Christians talk of universal brotherhood; but anyone who is not a Christian must go to that place where he will be eternally barbecued. (CW, 2:379-80)

71. Sin of Killing Cow

A man had laid out a beautiful garden into which a cow strayed one day and did much injury. The man in rage gave some blows to the cow which killed her. Then to avoid the terrible sin he bethought himself of a trick; knowing that Indra was the presiding deity of the hand, he tried to lay the blame on him.

Indra perceiving his sophistry appeared on the scene in the guise of a Brahmin and by a number of questions drew from him the answer that each and every item in connection with that garden was the man's own handiwork; whereupon Indra exposed his cunning with the cutting remark, 'Well, everything here has been done by you, and Indra alone is responsible for the killing of the cow, eh!' (CW, 7:127)

72. So He Has Also Followed Suit

A certain young man of little understanding used always to blame the Hindu Shastras before Sri Ramakrishna. One day he praised the Bhagavad Gita, on which Sri Ramakrishna said, 'Methinks, some European

Pandit has praised the Gita, and so he has also followed suit.' (CW, 4:477-78)

73. Who Serves the Lord the Best

A rich man had a garden and two gardeners. One of these gardeners was very lazy and did not work; but when the owner came to the garden, the lazy man would get up and fold his arms and say, 'How beautiful is the face of my master,' and dance before him.

The other gardener would not talk much, but would work hard, and produce all sorts of fruits and vegetables which he would carry on his head to his master who lived a long way off.

Of these two gardeners, which would be the more beloved of his master? Shiva is that master, and this world is His garden, and there are two sorts of gardeners here; the one who is lazy, hypocritical, and does nothing, only talking about Shiva's beautiful eyes and nose and other features; and the other, who is taking care of Shiva's children, all those that are poor and weak, all animals, and all His creation. Which of these would be the more beloved of Shiva? Certainly he that serves His children. He who wants to serve the father must serve the children first. He who wants to serve Shiva must serve His children—must serve all creatures in this world first. It is said in the Shastra that those who serve the servants of God are His greatest servants. So you will bear this in mind. (CW, 3:142)

74. It is the Heart that Moves, Truly

You may make thousands of societies, twenty thousand political assemblages, fifty thousand institutions. These will be of no use until there is that sympathy, that love, that heart that thinks for all; until Buddha's heart comes once more into India, until the words of the Lord Krishna are brought to their practical use, there is no hope for us. You go on imitating the Europeans and their societies and their assemblages, but let me tell you a story, a fact that I saw with my own eyes.

A company of Burmans was taken over to London by some persons here, who turned out to be Eurasians. They exhibited these people in London, took all the money, and then took these Burmans over to the Continent, and left them there for good or evil. These poor people did not know a word of any European language, but the English Consul in Austria sent them over to London. They were helpless in London, without knowing anyone. But an English lady got to know of them, took these foreigners from Burma into her own house, gave them her own clothes, her bed, and everything, and then sent the news to the papers. And, mark you, the next day the whole nation was, as it were, roused. Money poured in, and these people were helped out and sent back to Burma.

On this sort of sympathy are based all their political and other institutions; it is the rock-foundation of love, for themselves at least. They may not love the world; and the Burmans may be their enemies, but in England, it goes without saying, there is this great love for their own people, for truth and justice and charity to the stranger at the door. I should be the most ungrateful man if I did not tell you how wonderfully and how hospitably I was received in every country in the West. Where is the heart here to build upon? No sooner do we start a little joint-stock company than we try to cheat each other, and the whole thing comes down with a crash. You talk of imitating the English and building up as big a nation as they are. But where are the foundations? Ours are only sand, and, therefore, the building comes down with a crash in no time. (CW, 3:429,430)

75. Strength is the Test

There is an old story of an astrologer who came to a king and said, 'You are going to die in six months.'

The king was frightened out of his wits and was almost about to die then and there from fear. But his minister was a clever man, and this man told the king that these astrologers were fools. The king would not believe him.

So the minister saw no other way to make the king see that they were fools but to invite the astrologer to the palace again. There he asked him if his calculations were correct. The astrologer said that there could not be a mistake, but to satisfy him he went through the whole of the calculations again and then said that they were perfectly correct. The king's face became livid.

The minister said to the astrologer, 'And when do you think that you will die?' 'In twelve years,' was the reply.

The minister quickly drew his sword and separated the astrologer's head from the body and said to the king, 'Do you see this liar? He is dead this moment.' (CW, 8:185)

76. Do Something Religious

I read somewhere in a funny book that an American vessel was being foundered in the sea; the men were desperate and as a last solace wanted some religious service being done. There was 'Uncle Josh' on board who was an elder in the Presbyterian Church. They all began to entreat, 'Do something religious, Uncle Josh! We are all going to die.'

Uncle Joseph took his hat in his hand and took up a collection on the spot! (CW, 8:342)

77. We are Lions, not Sheep

Shall we advise men to kneel down and cry, 'O miserable sinners that we are!' No, rather let us remind them of their divine nature. I will tell you a story.

A lioness in search of prey came upon a flock of sheep, and as she jumped at one of them, she gave birth to a cub and died on the spot. The young lion was brought up in the flock, ate grass, and bleated like a sheep, and it never knew that it was a lion. One day a lion came across the flock and was astonished to see in it a huge lion eating grass and bleating like a sheep. At his sight the flock fled and the lion-sheep with them. But the lion watched his opportunity and one day found the lion-sheep asleep.

He woke him up and said, 'You are a lion.'

The other said, 'No,' and began to bleat like a sheep.

But the stranger lion took him to a lake and asked him to look in the water at his own image and see if it did not resemble him, the stranger lion. He looked and acknowledged that it did. Then the stranger lion began to roar and asked him to do the same. The lion-sheep tried his voice and was soon roaring as grandly as the other. And he was a sheep no longer.

My friends, I would like to tell you all that you are mighty as lions.

If the room is dark, do you go about beating your chest and crying, 'It is dark, dark, dark!' No, the only way to get the light is to strike a light, and then the darkness goes. The only way to realise the light above you is to strike the spiritual light within you, and the darkness of sin and impurity will flee away. (CW, 1:326-27)

SELF-REALIZATION

78. Satyakama's Story

I will relate to you a very ancient story from the Chandogya Upanishad, which tells how knowledge came to a boy. The form of the story is very crude, but we shall find that it contains a principle.

A young boy said to his mother, 'I am going to study the Vedas. Tell me the name of my father and my caste.'

The mother was not a married woman, and in India the child of a woman who has not been married is considered an outcast; he is not recognised by society and is not entitled to study the Vedas.

So the poor mother said, 'My child, I do not know your family name; I was in service, and served in different places; I do not know who your father is, but my name is Jabala and your name is Satyakama.'

The little child went to a sage and asked to be taken as a student. The sage asked him, 'What is the name of your father, and what is your caste?'

The boy repeated to him what he had heard from his mother.

The sage at once said, 'None but a Brahmin could speak such a damaging truth about himself. You are a Brahmin and I will teach you. You have not swerved from the truth.' So he kept the boy with him and educated him.

Now come some of the peculiar methods of education in ancient India. This teacher gave Satyakama four hundred lean, weak cows to take care of, and sent him to

139

the forest. There he went and lived for some time. The teacher had told him to come back when the herd would increase to the number of one thousand.

After a few years, one day Satyakama heard a big bull in the herd saying to him, 'We are a thousand now; take us back to your teacher. I will teach you a little of Brahman.'

'Say on, sir,' said Satyakama.

Then the bull said, 'The East is a part of the Lord, so is the West, so is the South, so is the North. The four cardinal points are the four parts of Brahman. Fire will also teach you something of Brahman.'

Fire was a great symbol in those days, and every student had to procure fire and make offerings. So on the following day, Satyakama started for his Guru's house, and when in the evening he had performed his oblation, and worshipped at the fire, and was sitting near it, he heard a voice come from the fire, 'O Satyakama.'

'Speak, Lord,' said Satyakama. (Perhaps you may remember a very similar story in the Old Testament, how Samuel heard a mysterious voice.)

'O Satyakama, I am come to teach you a little of Brahman. This earth is a portion of

that Brahman. The sky and heaven are portions of It. The
ocean is a part of that Brahman.'

Then the fire said that a certain bird would also teach
him something.

Satyakama continued his journey and on the next
day when he had performed his evening sacrifice a swan
came to him and said, 'I will teach you something about
Brahman. This fire which you worship, O Satyakama, is
a part of that Brahman. The sun is a part, the moon is a
part, the lightning is a part of that Brahman. A bird called
Madgu will tell you more about it.'

The next evening that bird came, and a similar voice
was heard by Satyakama, 'I will tell you something about
Brahman. Breath is a part of Brahman, sight is a part,
hearing is a part, the mind is a part.'

Then the boy arrived at his teacher's place and presented himself before him with due reverence.

No sooner had the teacher seen this disciple than
he remarked: 'Satyakama, thy face shines like that of a
knower of Brahman! Who then has taught thee?'

'Beings other than men,' replied Satyakama.

'But I wish that you should teach me, sir. For I have
heard from men like you that knowledge which is learnt
from a Guru alone leads to the supreme good.'

Then the sage taught him the same knowledge which
he had received from the gods. 'And nothing was left out,
yea, nothing was left out.' (CW, 2:309-11)

79. How Upakosala Got Knowledge

The next story belongs to Upakosala Kamalayana, a
disciple of this Satyakama, who went to be taught by
him and dwelt with him for some time.

Now Satyakama went away on a journey, and the student became very down-hearted; and when the teacher's wife came and asked him why he was not eating, the boy said, 'I am too unhappy to eat.' Then a voice came from the fire he was worshipping, saying 'This life is Brahman, Brahman is the ether, and Brahman is happiness. Know Brahman.'

'I know, sir,' the boy replied, 'that life is Brahman, but that It is ether and happiness I do not know.'

Then it explained that the two words ether and happiness signified one thing in reality, viz the sentient ether (pure intelligence) that resides in the heart. So, it taught him Brahman as life and as the ether in the heart.

Then the fire taught him, 'This earth, food, fire, and sun whom you worship, are forms of Brahman. The person that is seen in the sun, I am He. He who knows this and meditates on Him, all his sins vanish and he has long life and becomes happy. He who lives in the cardinal points, the moon, the stars, and the water, I am He. He who lives in this life, the ether, the heavens, and the lightning, I am He.' Here too we see the same idea of practical religion. The things which they were worshipping, such as the fire, the sun, the moon, and so forth, and the voice with which they were familiar, form the subject of the stories which explain them and give them a higher meaning.

And this is the real, practical side of Vedanta. It does not destroy the world, but it explains it; it does not destroy the person, but explains him; it does not destroy the individuality, but explains it by showing the real individuality. It does not show that this world is vain and does not exist, but it says, 'Understand what this world is, so that it may not hurt you.'

The voice did not say to Upakosala that the fire which

he was worshipping, or the sun, or the moon, or the lightning, or anything else, was all wrong, but it showed him
that the same spirit which was inside the sun, and the
moon, and lightning, and the fire, and the earth, was in
him, so that everything became transformed, as it were,
in the eyes of Upakosala. The fire which was merely a material fire before, in which to make oblations, assumed a
new aspect and became the Lord. The earth became transformed, life became transformed, the sun, the moon, the
stars, the lightning, everything became transformed and
deified. Their real nature was known. (CW, 2:311-12)

80. 'You Have Known the Truth'

There was a great sage in India called Vyasa. This
Vyasa is known as the author of the Vedanta aphor-
isms, and was a holy man. His father had tried to become a very perfect man and had failed. His grandfather
had also tried and failed. His great-grandfather had similarly tried and failed.

He himself did not succeed perfectly, but his son,
Shuka, was born perfect. Vyasa taught his son wisdom;
and after teaching him the knowledge of truth himself, he
sent him to the court of King Janaka. He was a great king
and was called Janaka Videha. Videha means 'without a
body'. Although a king, he had entirely forgotten that he
was a body; he felt that he was a spirit all the time. This
boy Shuka was sent to be taught by him.

The king knew that Vyasa's son was coming to him
to learn wisdom: so he made certain arrangements be-
forehand. And when the boy presented himself at the
gates of the palace, the guards took no notice of him
whatsoever. They only gave him a seat, and he sat there

for three days and nights, nobody speaking to him, nobody asking him who he was or whence he was. He was the son of a very great sage, his father was honoured by the whole country, and he himself was a most respectable person; yet the low, vulgar guards of the palace would take no notice of him.

After that, suddenly, the ministers of the king and all the big officials came there and received him with the greatest honours. They conducted him in and showed him into splendid rooms, gave him the most fragrant baths and wonderful dresses, and for eight days they kept him there in all kinds of luxury. That solemnly serene face of Shuka did not change even to the smallest extent by the change in the treatment accorded to him; he was the same in the midst of this luxury as when waiting at the door.

Then he was brought before the king. The king was on his throne, music was playing, and dancing and other amusements were going on. The king then gave him a cup of milk, full to the brim, and asked him to go seven times round the hall without spilling even a drop. The boy took the cup and proceeded in the midst of the music and the attraction of the beautiful faces. As desired by the king, seven times did he go round, and not a drop of the milk was spilt. The boy's mind could not be attracted by anything in the world, unless he allowed it to affect him.

And when he brought the cup to the king, the king said to him, 'What your father has taught you, and what you have learned yourself, I can only repeat. You have known the Truth; go home.'(CW, 1:90-92)

81. Gods and Demons

A god and a demon went to learn about the Self from a great sage. They studied with him for a long time. At last the sage told them, 'You yourselves are the Being you are seeking.'

Both of them thought that their bodies were the Self. They went back to their people quite satisfied and said, 'We have learned everything that was to be learned; eat, drink, and be merry; we are the Self; there is nothing beyond us.'

The nature of the demon was ignorant, clouded; so he never inquired any further, but was perfectly contented with the idea that he was God, that by the Self was meant the body.

The god had a purer nature. He at first committed the mistake of thinking: I, this body, am Brahman: so keep it strong and in health, and well dressed, and give it all sorts of enjoyments. But, in a few days, he found out that that could not be the meaning of the sage, their master; there must be something higher.

So he came back and said, 'Sir, did you teach me that this body was the Self? If so, I see all bodies die; the Self cannot die.'

The sage said, 'Find it out; thou art That.'

Then the god thought that the vital forces which work the body were what the sage meant. But, after a time, he found that if he ate, these vital forces remained strong, but, if he starved, they became weak.

The god then went back to the sage and said, 'Sir, do you mean that the vital forces are the Self?'

The sage said, 'Find out for yourself; thou art That.'

The god returned home once more, thinking that it was the mind, perhaps, that was the Self. But in a short while he saw that thoughts were so various, now good, again bad; the mind was too changeable to be the Self.

He went back to the sage and said, 'Sir, I do not think that the mind is the Self; did you mean that?'

'No,' replied the sage, 'thou art That; find out for yourself.'

The god went home, and at last found that he was the Self, beyond all thought, one without birth or death, whom the sword cannot pierce or the fire burn, whom the air cannot dry or the water melt, the beginningless and endless, the immovable, the intangible, the omniscient, the omnipotent Being; that It was neither the body nor the mind, but beyond them all. So he was satisfied; but the poor demon did not get the truth, owing to his fondness for the body.

This world has a good many of these demonic natures, but there are some gods too. If one proposes to teach any science to increase the power of sense-enjoyment, one finds multitudes ready for it. If one undertakes to show the supreme goal, one finds few to listen to him. Very few have the power to grasp the higher, fewer still the patience to attain to it. (CW, 1:140-42)

82. A Fable About Buddha

When Buddha was born, he was so pure that whosoever looked at his face from a distance immediately gave up the ceremonial religion and became a monk and became saved. So the gods held a meeting. They said, 'We are undone.' Because most of the gods live upon the ceremonials. These sacrifices go to the gods and these sacrifices were all gone. The gods were dying of hunger and [the reason for] it was that their power was gone.

So the gods said: 'We must, anyhow, put this man down. He is too pure for our life.'

And then the gods came and said: 'Sir, we come to ask you something. We want to make a great sacrifice and we mean to make a huge fire, and we have been seeking all over the world for a pure spot to light the fire on and could not find it, and now we have found it. If you will lie down, on your breast we will make the huge fire.'

'Granted,' he says, 'go on.'

And the gods built the fire high upon the breast of Buddha, and they thought he was dead, and he was not. And then they went about and said, 'We are undone.'

And all the gods began to strike him. No good. They could not kill him.

From underneath the voice comes: 'Why [are you] making all these vain attempts?'

'Whoever looks upon you becomes purified and is saved, and nobody is going to worship us.'

'Then, your attempt is vain, because purity can never be killed.'

This fable was written by his enemies, and yet throughout the fable the only blame that attaches to Buddha is that he was so great a teacher of purity. (CW, 3:525)

83. Yajnavalkya and Maitreyi

Yajnavalkya was a great sage. You know, the Shastras in India enjoin that every man should give up the world when he becomes old.

So Yajnavalkya said to his wife, 'My beloved, here is all my money, and my possessions, and I am going away.'

She replied, 'Sir, if I had this whole earth full of wealth, would that give me immortality?'

Yajnavalkya said, 'No, it will not. You will be rich, and that will be all, but wealth cannot give us immortality.'

She replied, 'What shall I do to gain that through which I shall become immortal? If you know, tell me.'

Yajnavalkya replied, 'You have been always my beloved; you are more beloved now by this question. Come, take your seat, and I will tell you; and when you have heard, meditate upon it.'

He said, 'It is not for the sake of the husband that the wife loves the husband, but for the sake of the Atman that she loves the husband, because she loves the Self. None loves the wife for the sake of the wife; but it is because one loves the Self that one loves the wife. None loves the children for the children; but because one loves the Self, therefore one loves the children. None loves wealth on account of the wealth; but because one loves the Self, therefore one loves wealth. None loves the Brahmin for the sake of the Brahmin; but because one loves the Self, one loves the Brahmin. So, none loves the Kshatriya for the sake of the Kshatriya, but because one loves the Self. Neither does any one love the world on account of the world, but because one loves the Self. None, similarly, loves the gods on account of the gods, but because one loves the Self. None loves a thing for that thing's sake; but it is for the Self that one loves it. This Self, therefore, is to be heard, reasoned about, and meditated upon. O my Maitreyi, when that Self has been heard, when that Self has been seen, when that Self has been realised, then, all this becomes known.'

What do we get then? Before us we find a curious philosophy. The statement has been made that every love is selfishness in the lowest sense of the word: because I love myself, therefore I love another; it cannot be. There have been philosophers in modern times who have said that self is the only motive power in the world. That is true, and yet it is wrong. But this self is but the shadow of that real Self which is behind. It appears wrong and evil because it is small. That infinite love for the Self, which is the universe, appears to be evil, appears to be small, because it appears through a small part. Even when the wife loves the husband, whether she knows it or not, she loves the husband for that Self. It is selfishness as it is manifested in the world, but that selfishness is really but a small part of that Self-ness. Whenever one loves, one has to love in and through the Self. This Self has to be known. What is the difference? Those that love the Self without knowing what It is, their love is selfishness. Those that love, knowing what that Self is, their love is free; they are sages.

'Him the Brahmin gives up who sees the Brahmin anywhere else but in the Self. Him the Kshatriya gives up who sees the Kshatriya anywhere else but in the Self. The world gives him up who sees this world anywhere but in that Atman. The gods give him up who loves the gods knowing them to be anywhere else but in the Atman. Everything goes away from him who knows everything as something else except the Atman. These Brahmins, these Kshatriyas, this world, these gods, whatever exists, everything is that Atman.'

Thus he explains what he means by love. Every time we particularise an object, we differentiate it from the Self. I am trying to love a woman; as soon as that woman is particularised, she is separated from the Atman, and my love for her will not be eternal, but will end in grief. But as soon as I see that woman as the Atman, that love becomes perfect, and will never suffer. So with everything; as soon as you are attached to anything in the universe, detaching it from the universe as a whole, from the Atman, there comes a reaction. With everything that we love outside the Self, grief and misery will be the result. If we enjoy everything in the Self, and as the Self, no misery or reaction will come. This is perfect bliss. How to come to this ideal?

Yajnavalkya goes on to tell us the process by which to reach that state. The universe is infinite: how can we take every particular thing and look at it as the Atman, without knowing the Atman? 'As with a drum when we are at a distance we cannot catch the sound, we cannot conquer the sound; but as soon as we come to the drum and put our hand on it, the sound is conquered. When the conch-shell is being blown, we cannot catch or conquer the sound, until we come near and get hold of the shell, and then it is conquered. When the Vina is being played, when we have come to the Vina, we get to the centre whence the sound is proceeding. As when some one is burning damp fuel, smoke and sparks of various kinds come, even so, from this great One has been breathed out knowledge; everything has come out of Him. He breathed out, as it were, all knowledge. As to all water, the one goal is the ocean; as to all touch, the skin is the one centre; as of all smell, the nose is the one centre; as to all taste, the tongue is the one goal; as of all form, the eyes are the one goal; as of all sounds, the ears are the one goal; as of all thought, the mind is the one goal; as of all knowledge, the heart is the one goal; as of all work, the hands are the one goal; as a morsel of salt put into the sea-water melts away, and we cannot take it back, even so, Maitreyi, is this Universal Being eternally infinite; all knowledge is in Him. The whole universe rises from Him, and again goes down into Him. No more is there any knowledge, dying or death.' We get the idea that we have all come just like sparks from Him, and when you know Him, then you go back and become one with Him again. We are the Universal.

Maitreyi became frightened, just as everywhere people become frightened. Said she, 'Sir, here is exactly where you have thrown a delusion over me. You have frightened me by saying there will be no more gods; all individuality will be lost. There will be no one to recognise, no one to love, no one to hate. What will become of us?'

'Maitreyi, I do not mean to puzzle you, or rather let it rest here. You may be frightened. Where there are two, one sees another, one hears another, one welcomes another, one thinks of another, one knows another. But when the whole has become that Atman, who is seen by whom, who is to be heard by whom, who is to be welcomed by whom, who is to be known by whom?'

That one idea was taken up by Schopenhauer and echoed in his philosophy. Through whom we know this universe, through what to know Him? How to know the knower? By what means can we know the knower? How can that be? Because in and through that we know everything. By what means can we know Him? By no means, for He is that means.

So far the idea is that it is all One Infinite Being. That is the real individuality, when there is no more division, and no more parts; these little ideas are very low, illusive. But yet in and through every spark of the individuality is shining that Infinite. Everything is a manifestation of the Atman. How to reach that?

First you make the statement, just as Yajnavalkya himself tells us: 'This Atman is first to be heard of.' So he stated the case; then he argued it out, and the last demon-

stration was how to know That, through which all knowledge is possible. Then, last, it is to be meditated upon. He
takes the contrast, the microcosm and the macrocosm,
and shows how they are rolling on in particular lines, and
how it is all beautiful. 'This earth is so blissful, so helpful
to every being; and all beings are so helpful to this earth:
all these are manifestations of that Self-effulgent One, the
Atman.'

All that is bliss, even in the lowest sense, is but the
reflection of Him. All that is good is His reflection, and
when that reflection is a shadow it is called evil. There are
no two Gods. When He is less manifested, it is called darkness, evil; and when He is more manifested, it is called
light. That is all. Good and evil are only a question of degree: more manifested or less manifested. Just take the
example of our own lives. How many things we see in our
childhood which we think to be good, but which really are
evil, and how many things seem to be evil which are good!
How the ideas change! How an idea goes up and up! What
we thought very good at one time we do not think so good
now. So good and evil are but superstitions, and do not
exist. The difference is only in degree. It is all a manifestation of that Atman; He is being manifested in everything;
only, when the covering is very thick we call it evil; and
when it is very thin, we call it good. It is the best, when all
covering goes away. So everything that is in the universe
is to be meditated upon in that sense alone, that we can
see it as all good, because it is the best. There is evil and
there is good; and the apex, the centre, is the Reality. He
is neither evil nor good; He is the best. The best can be
only one, the good can be many and the evil many. There
will be degrees of variation between the good and the evil,
but the best is only one, and that best, when seen through

thin coverings, we call different sorts of good, and when through thick covers, we call evil. Good and evil are different forms of superstition. They have gone through all sorts of dualistic delusion and all sorts of ideas, and the words have sunk into the hearts of human beings, terrorising men and women and living there as terrible tyrants. They make us become tigers. All the hatred with which we hate others is caused by these foolish ideas which we have imbibed since our childhood—good and evil. Our judgment of humanity becomes entirely false; we make this beautiful earth a hell; but as soon as we can give up good and evil, it becomes a heaven.

'This earth is blissful ('sweet' is the literal translation) to all beings and all beings are sweet to this earth; they all help each other. And all the sweetness is the Atman, that effulgent, immortal One who is inside this earth.'

Whose is this sweetness? How can there be any sweetness but He? That one sweetness is manifesting itself in various ways. Wherever there is any love, any sweetness in any human being, either in a saint or a sinner, either in an angel or a murderer, either in the body, mind, or the senses, it is He. Physical enjoyments are but He, mental enjoyments are but He, spiritual enjoyments are but He. How can there be anything but He? How can there be twenty thousand gods and devils fighting with each other? Childish dreams! Whatever is the lowest physical enjoyment is He, and the highest spiritual enjoyment is He. There is no sweetness but He. Thus says Yajnavalkya.

When you come to that state and look upon all things with the same eye, when you see even in the drunkard's pleasure in drink only that sweetness, then you have got the truth, and then alone you will know what happiness means, what peace means, what love means; and so long as you make these vain distinctions, silly, childish, foolish superstitions, all sorts of misery will come. But that immortal One, the effulgent One, He is inside the earth, it is all His sweetness, and the same sweetness is in the body.

This body is the earth, as it were, and inside all the powers of the body, all the enjoyments of the body, is He; the eyes see, the skin touches; what are all these enjoyments? That Self-effulgent One who is in the body, He is the Atman. This world, so sweet to all beings, and every being so sweet to it, is but the Self-effulgent; the Immortal is the bliss in that world. In us also, He is that bliss. He is the Brahman. 'This air is so sweet to all beings, and all beings are so sweet to it. But He who is that Self-effulgent Immortal Being in the air—is also in this body. He is expressing Himself as the life of all beings. This sun is so sweet to all beings. All beings are so sweet to this sun. He who is the Self-effulgent Being in the sun, we reflect Him as the smaller light. What can be there but His reflection? He is in the body, and it is His reflection which makes us see the light. This moon is so sweet to all, and every one is so sweet to the moon, but that Self-effulgent and Immortal One who is the soul of that moon, He is in us expressing Himself as mind. This lightning is so beautiful, every one is so sweet to the lightning, but the Self-effulgent and Immortal One is the soul of this lightning, and is also in us, because all is that Brahman. The Atman, the Self, is the king of all beings.' These ideas are very helpful to men; they are for meditation. For instance, meditate on the earth; think of the earth and at the same time know that we have That which is in the earth, that both are the same. Identify the body with the earth, and identify the soul with the Soul behind. Identify the air with the soul that is in the air and that is in me. They are all one, manifested in different forms.

To realise this unity is the end and aim of all meditation, and this is what Yajnavalkya was trying to explain to Maitreyi. (CW, 2:416-22)

84. The Story of Vedanta

A little love awoke in the hearts of mankind. It was very small indeed, and even now it is not much greater. It was at first confined to a tribe embracing perhaps members of the same tribe; these gods loved their tribes and each god was a tribal god, and the protector of that tribe. And sometimes the members of a tribe would think of themselves as the descendants of their god, just as the clans in different nations think that they are the common descendants of the man who was the founder of the clan.

There were in ancient times, and are even now, some people who claim to be descendants not only of these tribal gods, but also of the Sun and the Moon. You read in the ancient Sanskrit books of the great heroic emperors of the solar and the lunar dynasties. They were first worshippers of the Sun and the Moon, and gradually came to think of themselves as descendants of the god of the Sun, of the Moon, and so forth. So when these tribal ideas began to grow there came a little love, some slight idea of duty towards each other, a little social organisation. Then, naturally, the idea came: How can we live together without bearing and forbearing? How can one man live with another without having some time or other to check his impulses, to restrain himself, to forbear from doing things which his mind would prompt him to do? It is impossible. Thus comes the idea of restraint. The whole social fabric is based upon the idea of restraint, and we all know that the man or woman who has not learnt the great lesson of bearing and forbearing leads a most miserable life.

Now, when the ideas of religion came, a glimpse or something higher, more ethical, dawned upon the intellect of mankind. The old gods were found to be incongruous— these boisterous, fighting, drinking, beef-eating gods of the ancients— whose delight was in the smell of burning flesh and libations of strong liquor. Sometimes Indra drank so much that he fell upon the ground and talked unintelligibly. These gods could no longer be tolerated. The notion had arisen of inquiring into motives, and the gods had to come in for their share of inquiry. Reason for such-and-such actions was demanded and the reason was wanting.

Therefore man gave up these gods, or rather they developed higher ideas concerning them. They took a survey, as it were, of all the actions and qualities of the gods and discarded those which they could not harmonise, and kept those which they could understand, and combined them, labelling them with one name, Deva-deva, the God of gods. The god to be worshipped was no more a simple symbol of power; something more was required than that. He was an ethical god; he loved mankind, and did good to mankind. But the idea of god still remained. They increased his ethical significance, and increased also his power. He became the most ethical being in the universe, as well as the most almighty.

But all this patchwork would not do. As the explanation assumed greater proportions, the difficulty which it sought to solve did the same. If the qualities of the god increased in arithmetical progression, the difficulty and doubt increased in geometrical progression. The difficulty of Jehovah was very little beside the difficulty of the God of the universe, and this question remains to the present day. Why under the reign of the almighty and all-loving God of the universe should diabolical things be allowed to remain? Why so much more misery than happiness, and so much more wickedness than good? We may shut our eyes to all these things, but the fact still remains that this world is a hideous world. At best, it is the hell of Tantalus.

Here we are with strong impulses and stronger cravings for sense-enjoyments, but cannot satisfy them. There rises a wave which impels us forward in spite of our own will, and as soon as we move one step, comes a blow. We are all doomed to live here like Tantalus. Ideals come into our head far beyond the limit of our sense-ideals, but when we seek to express them, we cannot do so.

On the other hand, we are crushed by the surging mass around us. Yet if I give up all ideality and merely struggle through this world, my existence is that of a brute, and I degenerate and degrade myself. Neither way is happiness. Unhappiness is the fate of those who are content to live in this world, born as they are. A thousand times greater misery is the fate of those who dare to stand forth for truth and for higher things and who dare to ask for something higher than mere brute existence here. These are facts; but there is no explanation—there cannot be any explanation. But the Vedanta shows the way out. You must bear in mind that I have to tell you facts that will frighten you sometimes, but if you remember what I say, think of it, and digest it, it will be yours, it will raise you higher, and make you capable of understanding and living in truth. (CW, 2:109-11)

85. The Story of Nachiketa

This [issue of Self] the Katha Upanishad speaks in very figurative language. There was, in ancient times, a very rich man, who made a certain sacrifice which required that he should give away everything that he had. Now, this man was not sincere. He wanted to get the fame and glory of having made the sacrifice, but he was only giving things which were of no further use to him—old cows, barren, blind, and lame.

He had a boy called Nachiketas. This boy saw that his father was not doing what was right, that he was breaking his vow; but he did not know what to say to him. In India, father and mother are living gods to their children. And so the boy approached the father with the greatest respect and humbly inquired of him, 'Father, to whom are you going to give me? For your sacrifice requires that everything shall be given away.'

The father was very much vexed at this question and replied, 'What do you mean, boy? A father giving away his own son?'

The boy asked the question a second and a third time, and then the angry father answered, 'Thee I give unto Death (Yama).'

And the story goes on to say that the boy went to Yama, the god of death. Yama was the first man who died. He went to heaven and became the governor of all the Pitris; all the good people who die, go, and live with him for a long time. He is very pure and holy person, chaste and good, as his name (Yama) implies.

So the boy went to Yama's world. But even gods are sometimes not at home, and three days this boy had to wait there.

After the third day Yama returned. 'O learned one,' said Yama, 'you have been waiting here for three days without food, and you are a guest worthy of respect. Salutation to thee, O Brahmin, and welfare to me! I am very sorry I was not at home. But for that I will make amends.

Ask three boons, one for each day.'

And the boy asked, 'My first boon is that my father's anger against me may pass away; that he will be kind to me and recognise me when you allow me to depart.' Yama granted this fully.

The next boon was that he wanted to know about a certain sacrifice which took people to heaven. Now we have seen that the oldest idea which we got in the Samhita portion of the Vedas was only about heaven where they had bright bodies and lived with the fathers. Gradually other ideas came, but they were not satisfying; there was still need for something higher. Living in heaven would not be very different from life in this world. At best, it would only be a very healthy rich man's life, with plenty of sense-enjoyments and a sound body which knows no disease. It would be this material world, only a little more refined; and we have seen the difficulty that the external material world can never solve the problem. So no heaven can solve the problem. If this world cannot solve the problem, no multiplication of this world can do so, because we must always remember that matter is only an infinitesimal part of the phenomena of nature. The vast part of phenomena which we actually see is not matter. For instance, in every moment of our life what a great part is played by thought and feeling, compared with the material phenomena outside! How vast is this internal world with its tremendous activity! The sense-phenomena are very small compared with it. The heaven solution commits this mistake; it insists that the whole of phenomena is only in touch, taste, sight, etc. So this idea of heaven did not give full satisfaction to all. Yet Nachiketas asks, as the second boon, about some sacrifice through which people might attain to this heaven. There was an idea in the Vedas that these sacrifices pleased the gods and took human beings to heaven.

In studying all religions you will notice the fact that whatever is old becomes holy. For instance, our forefathers in India used to write on birch bark, but in time they learnt how to make paper. Yet the birch bark is still looked upon as very holy. When the utensils in which they used to cook in ancient times were improved upon, the old ones became holy; and nowhere is this idea more kept up than in India. Old methods, which must be nine or ten thousand years old, as of rubbing two sticks together to make fire, are still followed. At the time of sacrifice no other method will do. So with the other branch of the Asiatic Aryans. Their modern descendants still like to obtain fire from lightning, showing that they used to get fire in this way. Even when they learnt other customs, they kept up the old ones, which then became holy. So with the Hebrews. They used to write on parchment. They now write on paper, but parchment is very holy. So with all nations. Every rite which you now consider holy was simply an old custom, and the Vedic sacrifices were of this nature. In course of time, as they found better methods of life, their ideas were much improved; still these old forms remained, and from time to time they were practised and received a holy significance.

Then, a body of men made it their business to carry on these sacrifices. These were the priests, who speculated on the sacrifices, and the sacrifices became everything to them. The gods came to enjoy the fragrance of the sacrifices, and it was considered that everything in this world could be got by the power of sacrifices. If certain oblations were made, certain hymns chanted, certain peculiar forms of altars made, the gods would grant everything. So

Nachiketas asks by what form of sacrifice a man can go to heaven. The second boon was also readily granted by Yama who promised that this sacrifice should henceforth be named after Nachiketas.

Then the third boon comes, and with that the Upanishad proper begins. The boy said, 'There is this difficulty: when a man dies some say he is, others that he is not. Instructed by you I desire to understand this.'

But Yama was frightened. He had been very glad to grant the other two boons.

Now he said, 'The gods in ancient times were puzzled on this point. This subtle law is not easy to understand. Choose some other boon, O Nachiketas, do not press me on this point, release me.'

The boy was determined, and said, 'What you have said is true, O Death, that even the gods had doubts on this point, and it is no easy matter to understand. But I cannot obtain another exponent like you and there is no other boon equal to this.'

Death said, 'Ask for sons and grandsons who will live one hundred years, many cattle, elephants, gold, and horses. Ask for empire on this earth and live as many years as you like. Or choose any other boon which you think equal to these—wealth and long life. Or be thou a king, O Nachiketas, on the wide earth. I will make thee the enjoyer of all desires. Ask for all those desires which are difficult to obtain in the world. These heavenly maidens with chariots and music, which are not to be obtained by man, are yours. Let them serve you, O Nachiketas, but do not question me as to what comes after death.'

Nachiketas said, 'These are merely things of a day, O Death, they wear away the energy of all the sense-organs. Even the longest life is very short. These horses and chariots, dances and songs, may remain with Thee. Man cannot be satisfied by wealth. Can we retain wealth when we behold Thee? We shall live only so long as Thou desirest. Only the boon which I have asked is chosen by me.'

Yama was pleased with this answer and said, 'Perfection is one thing and enjoyment another; these two having different ends, engage men differently. He who chooses perfection becomes pure. He who chooses enjoyment misses his true end. Both perfection and enjoyment present themselves to man; the wise man having examined both distinguishes one from the other. He chooses perfection as being superior to enjoyment, but the foolish man chooses enjoyment for the pleasure of his body. O Nachiketas, having thought upon the things which are only apparently desirable, thou hast wisely abandoned them.' Death then proceeded to teach Nachiketas.

We now get a very developed idea of renunciation and Vedic morality, that until one has conquered the desires for enjoyment the truth will not shine in him. So long as these vain desires of our senses are clamouring and as it were dragging us outwards every moment, making us slaves to everything outside—to a little colour, a little taste, a little touch—notwithstanding all our pretensions, how can the truth express itself in our hearts?

Yama said, 'That which is beyond never rises before the mind of a thoughtless child deluded by the folly of riches. 'This world exists, the other does not,' thinking thus they come again and again under my power. To understand this truth is very difficult. Many, even hearing it continually, do not understand it, for the speaker must be wonderful, so must the hearer. The teacher must be wonderful, so must be the taught. Neither is the mind to be disturbed by vain arguments, for it is no more a question of argument, it is a question of fact.'...This is the watchword of Vedanta—realise religion, no talking will do. ...

You have all heard of that rich man in Rome who learnt one day that he had only about a million pounds of his property left; he said, 'What shall I do tomorrow?' and forthwith committed suicide. A million pounds was poverty to him. What is joy, and what is sorrow? It is a vanishing quantity, continually vanishing. When I was a child I thought if I could be a cabman, it would be the very acme of happiness for me to drive about. I do not think so now. To what joy will you cling? This is the one point we must all try to understand, and it is one of the last superstitions to leave us. Everyone's idea of pleasure is different. I have seen a man who is not happy unless he swallows a lump of opium every day. He may dream of a heaven where the land is made of opium. That would be a very bad heaven for me. Again and again in Arabian poetry we read of heaven with beautiful gardens, through which rivers run. I lived much of my life in a country where there is too much water; many villages are flooded and thousands of lives are sacrificed every year.

So, my heaven would not have gardens through which rivers flow; I would have a land where very little rain falls. Our pleasures are always changing. If a young man dreams of heaven, he dreams of a heaven where he will have a beautiful wife. When that same man becomes old he does not want a wife. It is our necessities which make our heaven, and the heaven changes with the change of our necessities. ...

'That which all the Vedas declare, which is proclaimed by all penances, seeking which men lead lives of continence, I will tell you in one word—it is 'Om'.' You will find this word 'Om' praised very much in the Vedas, and it is held to be very sacred.

Now Yama answers the question: 'What becomes of a man when the body dies?'

'This Wise One never dies, is never born, It arises from nothing, and nothing arises from It. Unborn, Eternal, Everlasting, this Ancient One can never be destroyed with the destruction of the body. If the slayer thinks he can slay, or if the slain thinks he is slain, they both do not know the truth, for the Self neither slays nor is slain.' A most tremendous position.

I should like to draw your attention to the adjective in the first line, which is 'wise'. As we proceed we shall find that the ideal of the Vedanta is that all wisdom and all purity are in the soul already, dimly expressed or better expressed—that is all the difference. The difference between man and man, and all things in the whole creation, is not in kind but only in degree. The background, the reality, of everyone is that same Eternal, Ever Blessed, Ever Pure, and Ever Perfect One. It is the Atman, the Soul, in the saint and the sinner, in the happy and the miserable, in the beautiful and the ugly, in men and in animals; it is the same throughout. It is the shining One. The difference is caused by the power of expression. In some It is expressed more, in others less, but this difference of expression has no effect upon the Atman. ...

'This Atman is not to be realised by the power of speech, nor by a vast intellect, nor by the study of the Vedas.' This is a very bold utterance. As I told you before, the sages were very bold thinkers, and never stopped at anything. You will remember that in India these Vedas are regarded in a much higher light than even the Christians regard their Bible. Your idea of revelation is that a man was inspired by God; but in India the idea is that things exist because they are in the Vedas. In and through the Vedas the whole creation has come. All that is called knowledge is in the Vedas. Every word is sacred and eternal, eternal as the soul, without beginning and without end. The whole of the Creator's mind is in this book, as it were. That is the light in which the Vedas are held. Why is this thing moral? Because the Vedas say so. Why is that thing immoral? Because the Vedas say so. In spite of that, look at the boldness of these sages who proclaimed that the truth is not to be found by much study of the Vedas. 'With whom the Lord is pleased, to that man He expresses Himself.' But then, the objection may be advanced that this is something like partisanship. But Yama explains, 'Those who are evil-doers, whose minds are not peaceful, can never see the Light. It is to those who are true in heart, pure in deed, whose senses are controlled, that this Self manifests Itself.'

Here is a beautiful figure. Picture the Self to be the rider and this body the chariot, the intellect to be the charioteer, mind the reins, and the senses the horses. He whose horses are well broken, and whose reins are strong and kept well in the hands of the charioteer (the intellect) reaches the goal which is the state of Him, the Omnipresent. But the man whose horses (the senses) are not controlled, nor the reins (the mind) well managed, goes to destruction. This Atman in all beings does not manifest Himself to the eyes or the senses, but those whose minds have become purified and refined realise Him. Beyond all sound, all sight, beyond form, absolute, beyond all taste and touch, infinite, without beginning and without end, even beyond nature, the Unchangeable; he who realises Him, frees himself from the jaws of death. But it is very difficult. It is, as it were, walking on the edge of a razor;

the way is long and perilous, but struggle on, do not despair. Awake, arise, and stop not till the goal is reached. ...
The great question that generally arises is the utility of philosophy. To that there can be only one answer: if on the utilitarian ground it is good for men to seek for pleasure, why should not those whose pleasure is in religious speculation seek for that? Because sense-enjoyments please many, they seek for them, but there may be others whom they do not please, who want higher enjoyment. The dog's pleasure is only in eating and drinking. The dog cannot understand the pleasure of the scientist who gives up everything, and, perhaps, dwells on the top of a mountain to observe the position of certain stars. The dogs may smile at him and think he is a madman. Perhaps this poor scientist never had money enough to marry even, and lives very simply. May be, the dog laughs at him.

But the scientist says, 'My dear dog, your pleasure is only in the senses which you enjoy, and you know nothing beyond; but for me this is the most enjoyable life, and if you have the right to seek your pleasure in your own way, so have I in mine.'

The mistake is that we want to tie the whole world down to our own plane of thought and to make our mind the measure of the whole universe. ... The misery in the world is like chronic rheumatism in the body; drive it from one part and it goes to another, drive it from there and you will feel it somewhere else. Whatever you do, it is still there. In olden times people lived in forests, and ate each other; in modern times they do not eat each other's flesh, but they cheat one another. Whole countries and cities are ruined by cheating. That does not show much progress. I do not see that what you call progress in the world is other than the multiplication of desires.

If one thing is obvious to me it is this that desires bring all misery; it is the state of the beggar, who is always begging for something, and unable to see anything without the wish to possess it, is always longing, longing for more. If the power to satisfy our desire is increasing in arithmetical progression, the power of desire is increased in geometrical progression. The sum total of happiness and misery in this world is at least the same throughout. If a wave rises in the ocean it makes a hollow somewhere. If happiness comes to one man, unhappiness comes to another or, perhaps, to some animal. Men are increasing in numbers and some animals are decreasing; we are killing them off, and taking their land; we are taking all means of sustenance from them. How can we say, then, that happiness is increasing? The strong race eats up the weaker, but do you think that the strong race will be very happy? No; they will begin to kill each other. I do not see on practical grounds how this world can become a heaven. Facts are against it. On theoretical grounds also, I see it cannot be.

... This world is nothing. It is at best only a hideous caricature, a shadow of the Reality. We must go to the Reality. Renunciation will take us to It. Renunciation is the very basis of our true life; every moment of goodness and real life that we enjoy is when we do not think of ourselves. This little separate self must die. Then we shall find that we are in the Real, and that Reality is God, and He is our own true nature, and He is always in us and with us. Let us live in Him and stand in Him. It is the only joyful state of existence. Life on the plane of the Spirit is the only life, and let us all try to attain to this realisation. (CW, 2: 157-74)

86. Nature is Like Ferris Wheel

You have seen the big Ferris Wheel in Chicago. The wheel revolves, and the little rooms in the wheel are regularly coming one after another; one set of persons gets into these, and after they have gone round the circle, they get out, and a fresh batch of people gets in. Each one of these batches is like one of these manifestations, from the lowest animals to the highest man. Nature is like the chain of the Ferris Wheel, endless and infinite, and these little carriages are the bodies or forms in which fresh batches of souls are riding, going up higher and higher until they become perfect and come out of the wheel. (CW, 2:230)

87. We Are Like Silkworms

We are like silkworms; we make the thread out of our own substance and spin the cocoon, and in course of time are imprisoned inside. But this is not for ever. In that cocoon we shall develop spiritual realisation, and like the butterfly come out free. (CW, 2:355)

88. The Intense Desire To Be Free

When the desire will arise to have a peaceful, quiet life, that shall come where everything shall be propitious for the development of the mind— you may take that as my experience. It may come after thousands of lives, but it must come. Hold on to that, the desire. You cannot have the strong desire if its object was not outside for you already. Of course, you must understand, there is a difference between desire and desire.

The master said, 'My child, if you desire after God, God shall come to you.'

The disciple did not understand his master fully. One day both went to bathe in a river, and the master said, 'Plunge in', and the boy did so. In a moment the master was upon him, holding him down. He would not let the boy come up.

When the boy struggled and was exhausted, he let him go. 'Yes, my child, how did you feel there?' 'Oh, the desire for a breath of air!'

'Do you have that kind of desire for God?'

'No, sir.'

'Have that kind of desire for God, and you shall have God.' (CW, 5:250-51)

89. 'Where Shall It Fall?'

In a certain school a number of little children were being examined. The examiner had foolishly put all sorts of difficult questions to the little children. Among others there was this question: 'Why does not the earth fall?' His intention was to bring out the idea of gravitation or some other intricate scientific truth from these children.

Most of them could not even understand the question, and so they gave all sorts of wrong answers. But one bright little girl answered it with another question: 'Where shall it fall?' The very question of the examiner was nonsense on the face of it. There is no up and down in the universe; the idea is only relative. So it is with regard to the soul; the very question of birth and death in regard to it is utter nonsense. Who goes and who comes? Where are you not? Where is the heaven that you are not in al-

ready? Omnipresent is the Self of man. Where is it to go? Where is it not to go? It is everywhere.

So all this childish dream and puerile illusion of birth and death, of heavens and higher heavens and lower worlds, all vanish immediately for the perfect. For the nearly perfect it vanishes after showing them the several scenes up to Brahmaloka. It continues for the ignorant. (CW, 2:277)

90. Eat the Mangoes

Bhagavan Ramakrishna used to tell a story of some men who went into a mango orchard and busied themselves in counting the leaves, the twigs, and the branches, examining their color, comparing their size and noting down everything most carefully, and then got up a learned discussion on each of these topics, which were undoubtedly highly interesting to them. But one of them, more sensible than the others, did not care for all these things, and instead thereof, began to eat the mango fruit. And was he not wise? So leave this counting of leaves and twigs and note-taking to others. This kind of work has its proper place, but not here in the spiritual domain. You never see a strong spiritual man among these 'leaf-counters'.

Religion, the highest aim, the highest glory of man, does not require so much labour. If you want to be a Bhakta, it is not at all necessary for you to know whether Krishna was born in Mathura or in Vraja, what he was doing, or just the exact date on which he pronounced the teachings of the Gita. You only require to feel the craving for the beautiful lessons of duty and love in the Gita. All the other particulars about it and its author are for the enjoyment of the learned. Let them have what they desire. Say 'Shantih, Shantih' to their learned controversies, and let us 'eat the mangoes.' (CW, 3:49-50)

91. The Passing Away of Buddha

Those last dying words of his always thrilled through my heart. He was old, he was suffering, he was near his death, and then came the despised outcaste—he lives on carrion, dead animals; the Hindus would not allow them to come into cities—one of these invited him to a dinner and he came with his disciples, and the poor Chanda, he wanted to treat this great teacher according to what he thought would be best; so he had a lot of pig's flesh and a lot of rice for him, and Buddha looked at that.

The disciples were all [hesitating], and the Master said: 'Well, do not eat, you will be hurt.' But he quietly sat down and ate. The teacher of equality must eat the [out-caste] Chanda's dinner, even the pig's flesh. He sat down and ate it.

He was already dying. He found death coming on, and he said, 'Spread for me something under this tree, for I think the end is near.'

And he was there under the tree, and he laid himself down; he could not sit up any more. And the first thing he did, he said: 'Go to that Chanda and tell him that he has been one of my greatest benefactors; for his meal, I am going to Nirvana.'

And then several men came to be instructed, and a disciple said, 'Do not go near now, the Master is passing away.'

And as soon as he heard it, the Lord said, 'Let them come in.'

And somebody else came and the disciples would not [let them enter]. Again they came, and then the dying Lord said: 'And O, thou Ananda, I am passing away. Weep not for me. Think not for me. I am gone. Work out diligently your own salvation. Each one of you is just what I am. I am nothing but one of you. What I am today is what I made myself. Do you struggle and make yourselves what I am. ...'

These are the memorable words of Buddha: 'Believe not because an old book is produced as an authority. Believe not because your father said [you should] believe the same. Believe not because other people like you believe it. Test everything, try everything, and then believe it, and if you find it for the good of many, give it to all.' And with these words, the Master passed away. (CW, 3:527-528)

92. Have You Seen God?

An ancient sage of the Upanishads sent his son out to learn about Brahman, and the child came back, and the father asked, 'What have you learnt?'

The child replied he had learnt so many sciences. But the father said, 'That is nothing, go back.'

And the son went back, and when he returned again the father asked the same question, and the same answer came form the child. Once more he had to go back. And the next time he came, his whole face was shining; and his father stood up and declared, 'Ay, today, my child, your face shines like a knower of Brahman.'

When you have known God, your very face will be changed, your voice will be changed, your whole appearance will be changed. You will be a blessing to mankind; none will be able to resist the rishi. This is the rishihood, the ideal in our religion. The rest, all these talks and reasonings and philosophies and dualisms and monisms, and even the Vedas themselves are but preparations, secondary things. The other is primary. (CW, 3:254)

93. 'Whosoever Will Save His Life'

A rich young man asked Jesus, 'Good Master, what shall I do that I may inherit eternal life?' And Jesus said unto him, 'One thing thou lackest; go thy way, sell whatsoever thou hast, and give to the poor, and thou shalt have treasures in heaven: and come, take up thy cross, and follow Me.' And he was sad at that saying and went away grieved; for he had great possessions. We are all more or less like that. The voice is ringing in our ears day and night. In the midst of our pleasures and joys, in the midst of worldly things, we think that we have forgotten everything else. Then comes a moment's pause and the voice rings in our ears: 'Give up all that thou hast and follow Me.' 'Whosoever will save his life shall lose it; and whosoever shall lose his life for My sake shall find it.' For whoever gives up this life for His sake, finds the life immortal. (CW, 4:149)

94. Buddha's Counsel

Buddhism is one of our sects. It was founded by a great man called Gautama, who became disgusted at the eternal metaphysical discussions of his day, and the cumbrous rituals, and more especially with the caste system. Some people say that we are born to a certain state, and therefore we are superior to others who are not thus born. He was also against the tremendous priestcraft. He preached a religion in which there was no motive power, and was perfectly agnostic about metaphysics or theories about God. He was often asked if there was a God, and he answered, he did not know. When asked about right conduct, he would reply, 'Do good and be good.'

There came five Brahmins, who asked him to settle their discussion. One said, 'Sir, my book says that God is such and such, and that this is the way to come to God.'

Another said, 'That is wrong, for my book says such and such, and this is the way to come to God'; and so the others. He listened calmly to all of them, and then asked them one by one, 'Does any one of your books say that God becomes angry, that He ever injures anyone, that He is impure?' 'No, Sir, they all teach that God is pure and good.' 'Then, my friends, why do you not become pure and good first, that you may know what God is?' (CW, 4:135)

MISCELLANEOUS

95. The Transformation

There was a young man that could not in any way support his family. He was strong and vigorous and, finally, became a highway robber; he attacked persons in the street and robbed them, and with that money he supported his father, mother, wife, and children. This went on continually, until one day a great saint called Narada was passing by, and the robber attacked him.

The sage asked the robber, 'Why are you going to rob me? It is a great sin to rob human beings and kill them. What do you incur all this sin for?'

The robber said, 'Why, I want to support my family with this money.'

'Now', said the sage, 'do you think that they take a share of your sin also?'

'Certainly they do,' replied the robber.

'Very good,' said the sage, 'make me safe by tying me up here, while you go home and ask your people whether they will share your sin in the same way as they share the money you make.'

The man accordingly went to his father, and asked, 'Father, do you know how I support you?'

He answered, 'No, I do not.' 'I am a robber, and I kill persons and rob them.'

'What! you do that, my son? Get away! You outcast!'

He then went to his mother and asked her, 'Mother, do you know how I support you?'

'No,' she replied. 'Through robbery and murder.'

'How horrible it is!' cried the mother.

'But, do you partake in my sin?' said the son.

'Why should I? I never committed a robbery,' answered the mother.

Then, he went to his wife and questioned her, 'Do you know how I maintain you all?'

'No,' she responded.

'Why, I am a highwayman,' he rejoined, 'and for years have been robbing people; that is how I support and maintain you all. And what I now want to know is, whether you are ready to share in my sin.'

'By no means. You are my husband, and it is your duty to support me.'

The eyes of the robber were opened. 'That is the way of the world—even my nearest relatives, for whom I have been robbing, will not share in my destiny.'

He came back to the place where he had bound the sage, unfastened his bonds, fell at his feet, recounted everything and said, 'Save me! What can I do?'

The sage said, 'Give up your present course of life. You see that none of your family really loves you, so give up all these delusions. They will share your prosperity; but the moment you have nothing, they will desert you. There is none who will share in your evil, but they will all share in your good. Therefore worship Him who alone stands by us whether we are doing good or evil. He never leaves us, for love never drags down, knows no barter, no selfishness.'

Then the sage taught him how to worship. And this man left everything and went into a forest. There he went on praying and meditating until he forgot himself so entirely that the ants came and built ant-hills around him, and he was quite unconscious of it.

After many years had passed, a voice came saying, 'Arise, O sage!'

Thus aroused he exclaimed, 'Sage? I am a robber!'

'No more 'robber',' answered the voice, 'a purified sage art thou. Thine old name is gone. But now, since thy meditation was so deep and great that thou didst not mark even the ant-hills which surrounded thee, henceforth, thy name shall be Valmiki—'he that was born in the ant-hill'.'

So, he became a sage. (CW, 4:63-65)

96. The Story of Ramayana

There are two great epics in the Sanskrit language, which are very ancient. Of course, there are hundreds of other epic poems. The Sanskrit language and literature have been continued down to the present day, although, for more than two thousand years, it has ceased to be a spoken language. I am now going to speak to you of the two most ancient epics, called the Ramayana and the Mahabharata. They embody the manners and customs, the state of society, civilisation, etc., of the ancient Indians. The oldest of these epics is called Ramayana, 'The Life of Rama'. There was some poetical literature before this—most of the Vedas, the sacred books of the Hindus, are written in a sort of metre—but this book is held by common consent in India as the very beginning of poetry.

The name of the poet or sage was Valmiki. Later on, a great many poetical stories were fastened upon that ancient poet; and subsequently, it became a very general practice to attribute to his authorship very many verses that were not his. Notwithstanding all these interpolations, it comes down to us as a very beautiful arrangement, without equal in the literatures of the world.

One day as this sage, Valmiki, was going to bathe in the holy river Ganga, he saw a pair of doves wheeling round and round, and kissing each other. The sage looked up and was pleased at the sight, but in a second an arrow whisked past him and killed the male dove. As the dove fell down on the ground, the female dove went on whirling round and round the dead body of its companion in grief. In a moment the poet became miserable, and looking round, he saw the hunter. 'Thou art a wretch,' he cried, 'without the smallest mercy! Thy slaying hand would not even stop for love!' 'What is this? What am I saying?' the poet thought to himself, 'I have never spoken in this sort of way before.' And then a voice came: 'Be not afraid. This is poetry that is coming out of your mouth. Write the life of Rama in poetic language for the benefit of the world.' And that is how the poem first began. The first verse sprang out of pity from the mouth of Valmiki, the first poet. And it was after that, that he wrote the beautiful Ramayana, 'The Life of Rama'.

There was an ancient Indian town called Ayodhya—and it exists even in modern times. The province in which it is still located is called Oudh, and most of you may have noticed it in the map of India. That was the ancient Ayodhya. There, in ancient times, reigned a king called Dasharatha. He had three queens, but the king had not any children by them. And like good Hindus, the king and the queens, all went on pilgrimages fasting and praying, that they might have children and, in good time, four sons were born. The eldest of them was Rama.

Now, as it should be, these four brothers were thoroughly educated in all branches of learning. To avoid future quarrels there was in ancient India a custom for the king in his own lifetime to nominate his eldest son as his successor, the Yuvaraja, young king, as he is called.

Now, there was another king, called Janaka, and this king had a beautiful daughter named Sita. Sita was found in a field; she was a daughter of the Earth, and was born without parents. The word 'Sita' in ancient Sanskrit means the furrow made by a plough. In the ancient mythology of India you will find persons born of one parent only, or persons born without parents, born of sacrificial fire, born in the field, and so on—dropped from the clouds as it were. All those sorts of miraculous births were common in the mythological lore of India.

Sita, being the daughter of the Earth, was pure and immaculate. She was brought up by King Janaka. When she was of a marriageable age, the king wanted to find a suitable husband for her.

There was an ancient Indian custom called Svayam-vara, by which the princesses used to choose husbands. A number of princes from different parts of the country were invited, and the princess in splendid array, with a garland in her hand, and accompanied by a crier who enu-merated the distinctive claims of each of the royal suitors, would pass in the midst of those assembled before her, and select the prince she liked for her husband by throw-ing the garland of flowers round his neck. They would then be married with much pomp and grandeur.

There were numbers of princes who aspired for the hand of Sita; the test demanded on this occasion was the breaking of a huge bow, called Haradhanu. All the princ-es put forth all their strength to accomplish this feat, but failed. Finally, Rama took the mighty bow in his hands and with easy grace broke it in twain. Thus Sita selected Rama, the son of King Dasharatha for her husband, and they were wedded with great rejoicings. Then, Rama took his bride to his home, and his old father thought that the time was now come for him to retire and appoint Rama as Yuvaraja. Everything was accordingly made ready for the ceremony, and the whole country was jubilant over the affair, when the younger queen Kaikeyi was reminded by one of her maid-servants of two promises made to her by the king long ago.

At one time she had pleased the king very much, and he offered to grant her two boons: 'Ask any two things in my power and I will grant them to you,' said he, but she made no request then. She had forgotten all about it; but the evil-minded maidservant in her employ began to work upon her jealousy with regard to Rama being installed on the throne, and insinuated to her how nice it would be for her if her own son had succeeded the king, until the queen was almost mad with jealousy. Then the servant suggested to her to ask from the king the two promised boons: one would be that her own son Bharata should be placed on the throne, and the other, that Rama should be sent to the forest and be exiled for fourteen years.

Now, Rama was the life and the soul of the old king and when this wicked request was made to him, he as a king felt he could not go back on his word. So he did not know what to do. But Rama came to the rescue and will-ingly offered to give up the throne and go into exile, so that his father might not be guilty of falsehood. So Rama went into exile for fourteen years, accompanied by his loving wife Sita and his devoted brother Lakshmana, who would on no account be parted from him.

The Aryans did not know who were the inhabitants of these wild forests. In those days the forest tribes they called 'monkeys', and some of the so-called 'monkeys', if unusually strong and powerful, were called demons.

So, into the forest, inhabited by demons and monkeys, Rama, Lakshmana, and Sita went. When Sita had offered to accompany Rama, he exclaimed, 'How can you, a princess, face hardships and accompany me into a forest full of unknown dangers!' But Sita replied, 'Wherever Rama goes, there goes Sita. How can you talk of `princess' and `royal birth' to me? I go before you!'

So, Sita went. And the younger brother, he also went with them. They penetrated far into the forest, until they reached the river Godavari. On the banks of the river they built little cottages, and Rama and Lakshmana used to hunt deer and collect fruits. After they had lived thus for some time, one day there came a demon giantess. She was the sister of the giant king of Lanka (Ceylon). Roaming through the forest at will, she came across Rama, and seeing that he was a very handsome man, she fell in love with him at once. But Rama was the purest of men, and also he was a married man; so of course he could not return her love. In revenge, she went to her brother, the giant king, and told him all about the beautiful Sita, the wife of Rama.

Rama was the most powerful of mortals; there were no giants or demons or anybody else strong enough to conquer him. So, the giant king had to resort to subterfuge. He got hold of another giant who was a magician and changed him into a beautiful golden deer; and the deer went prancing round about the place where Rama lived, until Sita was fascinated by its beauty and asked Rama to go and capture the deer for her. Rama went into the forest to catch the deer, leaving his brother in charge of Sita.

Then Lakshmana laid a circle of fire round the cottage, and he said to Sita, 'Today I see something may befall you; and, therefore, I tell you not to go outside of this magic circle. Some danger may befall you if you do.' In the meanwhile, Rama had pierced the magic deer with his arrow, and immediately the deer, changed into the form of a man, died.

Immediately, at the cottage was heard the voice of Rama, crying, 'Oh, Lakshmana, come to my help!' and Sita said, 'Lakshmana, go at once into the forest to help Rama!' 'That is not Rama's voice,' protested Lakshmana.

But at the entreaties of Sita, Lakshmana had to go in search of Rama. As soon as he went away, the giant king, who had taken the form of a mendicant monk, stood at the gate and asked for alms. 'Wait awhile,' said Sita, 'until my husband comes back and I will give you plentiful alms.'

'I cannot wait, good lady,' said he, 'I am very hungry, give me anything you have.'

At this, Sita, who had a few fruits in the cottage, brought them out. But the mendicant monk after many persuasions prevailed upon her to bring the alms to him, assuring her that she need have no fear as he was a holy person. So Sita came out of the magic circle, and immediately the seeming monk assumed his giant body, and grasping Sita in his arms he called his magic chariot, and putting her therein, he fled with the weeping Sita. Poor Sita! She was utterly helpless, nobody was there to come to her aid. As the giant was carrying her away, she took off a few of the ornaments from her arms and at intervals dropped them to the ground.

She was taken by Ravana to his kingdom, Lanka, the island of Ceylon. He made proposals to her to become his queen, and tempted her in many ways to accede to his request. But Sita was chastity itself, would not even speak to the giant; and he to punish her, made her live under a tree, day and night, until she should consent to be his wife.

When Rama and Lakshmana returned to the cottage and found that Sita was not there, their grief knew no bounds. They could not imagine what had become of her. The two brothers went on, seeking, seeking everywhere for Sita, but could find no trace of her. After long searching, they came across a group of 'monkeys', and in the midst of them was Hanuman, the 'divine monkey'. Hanuman, the best of monkeys, became the most faithful servant of Rama and helped him in rescuing Sita, as we shall see later on. His devotion to Rama was so great that he is worshipped by the Hindus as the ideal of a true servant of the Lord. You see, by the 'monkeys' and 'demons' are meant the aborigines of South India.

So, Rama, at last, fell in with these monkeys. They told him that they had seen flying through the sky a chariot, in which was seated a demon who was carrying away a most beautiful lady, and that she was weeping bitterly, and as the chariot passed over their heads she dropped one of her ornaments to attract their attention.

Then they showed Rama the ornament. Lakshmana took up the ornament, and said, 'I do not know whose ornament this is.' Rama took it from him and recognised it at once, saying 'Yes, it is Sita's.'

Lakshmana could not recognise the ornament, because in India the wife of the elder brother was held in so much reverence that he had never looked upon the arms and the neck of Sita. So you see, as it was a necklace, he did not know whose it was. There is in this episode a touch of the old Indian custom.

Then, the monkeys told Rama who this demon king was, and where he lived, and then they all went to seek for him. Now, the monkey-king Vali and his younger brother Sugriva were then fighting amongst themselves for the kingdom. The younger brother was helped by Rama, and he regained the kingdom for Vali, who had driven him away; and he, in return, promised to help Rama. They searched the country all round, but could not find Sita. At last Hanuman leaped by one bound from the coast of India to the island of Ceylon, and there went looking all over Lanka for Sita, but nowhere could he find her.

You see, this giant king had conquered the gods, the men, in fact the whole world; and he had collected all the beautiful women and made them his concubines. So, Hanuman thought to himself, 'Sita cannot be with them in the palace. She would rather die than be in such a place.' So Hanuman went to seek for her elsewhere. At last, he found Sita under a tree, pale and thin, like the new moon that lies low in the horizon. Now Hanuman took the form of a little monkey and settled on the tree, and there he witnessed how giantesses sent by Ravana came and tried to frighten Sita into submission, but she would not even listen to the name of the giant king.

Then, Hanuman came nearer to Sita and told her how he became the messenger of Rama, who had sent him to find out where Sita was; and Hanuman showed to Sita the signet ring which Rama had given as a token for establishing his identity. He also informed her that as soon as Rama would know her whereabouts, he would come with an army and conquer the giant and recover her. However, he suggested to Sita that if she wished it, he would take her on his shoulders and could with one leap clear the ocean and get back to Rama. But Sita could not bear the idea, as she was chastity itself, and could not touch the body of any man except her husband. So, Sita remained where she was. But she gave him a jewel from her hair to carry to Rama; and with that Hanuman returned.

Learning everything about Sita from Hanuman, Rama collected an army, and with it marched towards the southernmost point of India. There Rama's monkeys built a huge bridge, called Setu-bandha, connecting India with Ceylon. In very low water even now it is possible to cross from India to Ceylon over the sand-banks there.

Now Rama was God incarnate, otherwise, how could he have done all these things? He was an Incarnation of God, according to the Hindus. They in India believe him to be the seventh Incarnation of God.

The monkeys removed whole hills, placed them in the sea and covered them with stones and trees, thus making a huge embankment. A little squirrel, so it is said, was there rolling himself in the sand and running backwards and forwards on to the bridge and shaking himself. Thus in his small way he was working for the bridge of Rama by putting in sand. The monkeys laughed, for they were bringing whole mountains, whole forests, huge loads of sand for the bridge—so they laughed at the little squirrel rolling in the sand and then shaking himself. But Rama saw it and remarked: 'Blessed be the little squirrel; he is doing his work to the best of his ability, and he is therefore quite as great as the greatest of you.' Then he gently stroked the squirrel on the back, and the marks of Rama's fingers, running lengthways, are seen on the squirrel's back to this day.

Now, when the bridge was finished, the whole army of monkeys, led by Rama and his brother entered Ceylon. For several months afterwards tremendous war and bloodshed followed. At last, this demon king, Ravana, was conquered and killed; and his capital, with all the palaces and everything, which were entirely of solid gold, was taken. In far-away villages in the interior of India, when I tell them that I have been in Ceylon, the simple folk say, 'There, as our books tell, the houses are built of gold.' So, all these golden cities fell into the hands of Rama, who gave them over to Vibhishana, the younger brother of Ravana, and seated him on the throne in the place of his brother, as a return for the valuable services rendered by him to Rama during the war.

Then Rama and Sita and his followers left Lanka. But there ran a murmur among his followers. 'The test! The test!' they cried, 'Sita has not given the test that she was perfectly pure in Ravana's household.'

'Pure! she is chastity itself!' exclaimed Rama.

'Never mind! We want the test,' persisted the people.

Subsequently, a huge sacrificial fire was made ready, into which Sita had to plunge herself. Rama was in agony, thinking that Sita was lost; but in a moment, the God of fire himself appeared with a throne upon his head, and upon the throne was Sita. Then, there was universal rejoicing, and everybody was satisfied.

Early during the period of exile, Bharata, the younger brother had come and informed Rama, of the death of the old king and vehemently insisted on his occupying the throne. During Rama's exile Bharata would on no account ascend the throne and out of respect placed a pair of Rama's wooden shoes on it as a substitute for his brother. Then Rama returned to his capital, and by the common consent of his people, he became the king of Ayodhya.

After Rama regained his kingdom, he took the necessary vows which in olden times the king had to take for the benefit of his people. The king was the slave of his people, he had to bow to public opinion, as we shall see later on. Rama passed a few years in happiness with Sita, when the people again began to murmur that Sita had been stolen by a demon and carried across the ocean. They were not satisfied with the former test and clamoured for another test, otherwise she must be banished.

In order to satisfy the demands of the people, Sita was banished, and left to live in the forest, where was the hermitage of the sage and poet Valmiki. The sage found poor Sita weeping and forlorn, and hearing her sad story, sheltered her in his ashrama. Sita was expecting soon to become a mother, and she gave birth to twin boys. The poet never told the children who they were. He brought them up together in the Brahmacharin life. He then composed the poem known as Ramayana, set it to music, and dramatised it.

The drama, in India, was a very holy thing. Drama and music are themselves held to be religion. Any song— whether it be a love-song or otherwise—if one's whole soul is in that song, one attains salvation, one has nothing else to do. They say it leads to the same goal as meditation.

So, Valmiki dramatised 'The Life of Rama', and taught Rama's two children how to recite and sing it.

There came a time when Rama was going to perform a huge sacrifice, or Yajna, such as the old kings used to celebrate. But no ceremony in India can be performed by a married man without his wife: he must have the wife with him, the Sahadharmini, the 'co-religionist'— that is the expression for the wife. The Hindu householder has to perform hundreds of ceremonies, but not one can be duly performed according to the Shastras, if he has not a wife to complement it with her part in it.

Now Rama's wife was not with him then, as she had been banished. So, the people asked him to marry again. But at this request Rama for the first time in his life stood against the people. He said, 'This cannot be. My life is Sita's.'

So, as substitute, a golden statue of Sita was made, in order that the ceremony could be accomplished. They arranged even a dramatic entertainment, to enhance the religious feeling of this great festival. Valmiki, the great sage-poet, came with his pupils, Lava and Kusha, the unknown sons of Rama. A stage had been erected and everything was ready for the performance. Rama and his brothers attended with all his nobles and his people—a vast audience. Under the direction of Valmiki, the life of Rama was sung by Lava and Kusha, who fascinated the whole assembly by their charming voice and appearance. Poor Rama was nearly maddened, and when in the drama, the scene of Sita's exile came about, he did not know what to do.

Then the sage said to him, 'Do not be grieved, for I will show you Sita.'

Then Sita was brought upon the stage and Rama delighted to see his wife. All of a sudden, the old murmur arose: 'The test! The test!' Poor Sita was so terribly overcome by the repeated cruel slight on her reputation that it was more than she could bear. She appealed to the gods to testify to her innocence, when the Earth opened and Sita exclaimed, 'Here is the test', and vanished into the bosom of the Earth. The people were taken aback at this tragic end. And Rama was overwhelmed with grief.

A few days after Sita's disappearance, a messenger came to Rama from the gods, who intimated to him that his mission on earth was finished and he was to return to heaven. These tidings brought to him the recognition of his own real Self. He plunged into the waters of the Sarayu, the mighty river that laved his capital, and joined Sita in the other world.

This is the great, ancient epic of India. Rama and Sita are the ideal of the Indian nation. All children, especially girls, worship Sita. The height of a woman's ambition is to be like Sita, the pure, the devoted, the all-suffering!

When you study these characters, you can at once find out how different is the ideal in India from that of the West. For the race, Sita stands as the ideal of suffering. The West says, 'Do! Show your power by doing.' India says, 'Show your power by suffering.' The West has solved the problem of how much a man can have: India has solved the problem of how little a man can have. The two extremes, you see. Sita is typical of India—the idealised India. (CW, 4:63-75)

97. The Danger of Frauds

Sometimes fraudulent people try to impose themselves upon mankind. In these days it is becoming all too prevalent. A friend of mine had a very fine picture. Another gentleman who was rather religiously inclined, and a rich man, had his eyes upon this picture; but my friend would not sell it. This other gentleman one day comes and says to my friend, I have an inspiration and I have a message from God. 'What is your message?' my friend asked. 'The message is that you must deliver that picture to me.' My friend was up to his mark; he immediately added, 'Exactly so; how beautiful! I had exactly the same inspiration, that I should have to deliver to you the picture. Have you brought your cheque?' 'Cheque? What cheque?'

'Then', said my friend, 'I don't think your inspiration was right. My inspiration was that I must give the picture to the man who brought a cheque for $100,000. You must bring the cheque first.'

The other man found he was caught, and gave up the

inspiration theory. These are the dangers. A man came to me in Boston and said he had visions in which he had been talked to in the Hindu language. I said, 'If I can see what he says I will believe it.'

But he wrote down a lot of nonsense. I tried my best to understand it, but I could not. I told him that so far as my knowledge went, such language never was and never will be in India. They had not become civilised enough to have such a language as that. He thought of course that I was a rogue and sceptic, and went away; and I would not be surprised next to hear that he was in a lunatic asylum. These are the two dangers always in this world—the danger from frauds, and the danger from fools. But that need not deter us, for all great things in this world are fraught with danger. (CW, 4:213-14)

98. A Leader Leads by Example

An English friend of mine, named General Strong, was in India during the Sepoy Mutiny. He used to tell many stories about it. One day, in the course of conversation, I asked him how it was that the sepoys who had enough of guns, ammunition, and provisions at their disposal, and were also trained veterans, came to suffer such a defeat.

He replied that the leaders among them, instead of advancing forward, only kept shouting from a safe position in the rear, 'Fight on, brave lads', and so forth; but unless the commanding officer goes ahead and faces death, the rank and file will never fight with heart. It is the same in every branch. 'A captain must sacrifice his head,' they say. If you can lay down your life for a cause, then only you can be a leader. But we all want to be leaders without mak-

ing the neces-
sary sacrifice.
And the result
is zero—no-

body listens to us!
(CW, 7:325-26)

99. Blind Men and Elephant

There was a procession in a village in India, and all the people turned out to see the procession, and specially the gaily caparisoned elephant. The people were delighted, and as the five blind men could not see, they determined to touch the elephant that they might acquaint themselves with its form. They were given the privilege, and after the procession had passed, they returned home together with the people, and they began to talk about the elephant.

'It was just like a wall,' said one.

'No it wasn't,' said another, 'it was like a piece of rope.'

'You are mistaken,' said a third, 'I felt him and it was just a serpent.'

The discussion grew excited, and the fourth declared the elephant was like a pillow. The argument soon broke into more angry expressions, and the five blind men took to fighting.

Along came a man with two eyes, and he said, 'My friends, what is the matter?' The disputation was explained, whereupon the new-comer said, 'Men, you are all right: the trouble is you touched the elephant at different points. The wall was the side, the rope was the tail, the serpent was the trunk, and the toes were the pillow. Stop your quarrelling; you are all right, only you have been viewing the elephant from different standpoints.' (CW, 7:416-17)

100. 'This is Fanaticism'

There are fanatics of various kinds. Some people are wine fanatics and cigar fanatics. Some think that if men gave up smoking cigars, the world would arrive at the millennium. Women are generally amongst these fanatics.

There was a young lady here one day, in this class. She was one of a number of ladies in Chicago who have built a house where they take in the working people and give them music and gymnastics. One day this young lady was talking about the evils of the world and said she knew the remedy.

I asked, 'How do you know?' and she answered, 'Have you seen Hull House?'

In her opinion, this Hull House is the one panacea for all the evils that flesh is heir to. This will grow upon her. I am sorry for her. There are some fanatics in India who think that if a woman could marry again when her husband died, it would cure all evil. This is fanaticism. (CW, 5:242)

101. The Greatest Birth

This human body is the greatest body in the universe, and a human being the greatest being. Man is higher than all animals, than all angels; none is greater than man. Even the Devas (gods) will have to come down again and attain to salvation through a human body. Man alone attains to perfection, not even the Devas. According to the Jews and Mohammedans, God created man after creating the angels and everything else, and after creating man He asked the angels to come and salute him, and all did so except Iblis; so God cursed him and he became Satan. Behind this allegory is the great truth that this human birth is the greatest birth we can have. (CW, 1:142)

102. Your Doctrine Of Heredity!

With all our boasted education of modern times, if anybody says a kind word for them, I often find our men shrink at once from the duty of lifting them up, these poor downtrodden people. Not only so, but I also find that all sorts of most demoniacal and brutal arguments, culled from the crude ideas of hereditary transmission and other such gibberish from the Western world, are brought forward in order to brutalise and tyrannise over the poor all the more.

At the Parliament of Religions in America, there came among others a young man, a born Negro, a real African Negro, and he made a beautiful speech. I became interested in the young man and now and then talked to him, but could learn nothing about him. But one day in England, I met some Americans; and this is what they told me. This boy was the son of a Negro chief who lived in the heart of

Africa, and that one day another chief became angry with the father of the boy and murdered him and murdered the mother also, and they were cooked and eaten; he ordered the child to be killed also and cooked and eaten; but the boy fled, and after passing through great hardships and having travelled a distance of several hundreds of miles, he reached the seashore, and there he was taken into an American vessel and brought over to America. And this boy made that speech! After that, what was I to think of your doctrine of heredity! (CW, 3:192-93)

103. The Story of Mahabharata

The other epic about which I am going to speak to you this evening, is called the Mahabharata. It contains the story of a race descended from King Bharata, who was the son of Dushyanta and Shakuntala. Maha means great, and Bharata means the descendants of Bharata, from whom India has derived its name, Bharata. Mahabharata means Great India, or the story of the great descendants of Bharata. The scene of this epic is the ancient kingdom of the Kurus, and the story is based on the great war which took place between the Kurus and the Panchalas. So the region of the quarrel is not very big. This epic is the most popular one in India; and it exercises the same authority in India as Homer's poems did over the Greeks. As ages went on, more and more matter was added to it, until it has become a huge book of about a hundred thousand couplets. All sorts of tales, legends and myths, philosophical treatises, scraps of history, and various discussions have been added to it from time to time, until it is a vast, gigantic mass of literature; and through it all runs the old, original story. The central story of the Mahabharata is of a war between two families of cousins, one family, called the Kauravas, the other the Pandavas—for the empire of India.

The Aryans came into India in small companies. Gradually, these tribes began to extend, until, at last, they became the undisputed rulers of India, and then arose this fight to gain the mastery, between two branches of the same family. Those of you who have studied the Gita know how the book opens with a description of the battle-field, with two armies arrayed one against the other. That is the war of the Mahabharata.

There were two brothers, sons of the emperor. The elder one was called Dhritarashtra, and the other was called Pandu. Dhritarashtra, the elder one, was born blind. According to Indian law, no blind, halt, maimed, consumptive, or any other constitutionally diseased person, can inherit. He can only get a maintenance. So, Dhritarashtra could not ascend the throne, though he was the elder son, and Pandu became the emperor.

Dhritarashtra had a hundred sons, and Pandu only had five. After the death of Pandu at an early age, Dhritarashtra became king of the Kurus and brought up the sons of Pandu along with his own children. When they grew up, they were placed under the tutorship of the great priest-warrior, Drona, and were well trained in the various material arts and sciences befitting princes. The education of the princes being finished, Dhritarashtra put Yudhishthira, the eldest of the sons of Pandu, on the throne of his father. The sterling virtues of Yudhishthira and the valour and devotion of his other brothers aroused jealousies in the hearts of the sons of the blind king, and at the instigation of Duryodhana, the eldest of them, the five Pandava brothers were prevailed upon to visit Varanavata, on the plea of a religious festival that was being held there.

There they were accommodated in a palace made under Duryodhana's instructions, of hemp, resin, and lac, and other inflammable materials, which were subsequently set fire to secretly. But the good Vidura, the stepbrother of Dhritarashtra, having become cognisant of the evil intentions of Duryodhana and his party, had warned the Pandavas of the plot, and they managed to escape without anyone's knowledge. When the Kurus saw the house was reduced to ashes, they heaved a sigh of relief and thought all obstacles were now removed out of their path. Then the children of Dhritarashtra got hold of the kingdom. The five Pandava brothers had fled to the forest with their mother, Kunti. They lived there by begging, and went about in disguise giving themselves out as Brahmana students. Many were the hardships and adventures they encountered in the wild forests, but their fortitude of mind, and strength, and valour made them conquer all dangers. So things went on until they came to hear of the approaching marriage of the princess of a neighbouring country.

I told you last night of the peculiar form of the ancient Indian marriage. It was called Svayamvara, that is, the choosing of the husband by the princess. A great gathering of princes and nobles assembled, amongst whom the princess would chose her husband. Preceded by her trumpeters and heralds she would approach, carrying a garland of flowers in her hand. At the throne of each candidate for her hand, the praises of that prince and all his great deeds in battle would be declared by the heralds. And when the princess decided which prince she desired to have for a husband, she would signify the fact by throwing the marriage-garland round his neck. Then the ceremony would turn into a wedding. King Drupada was a great king, king of the Panchalas, and his daughter, Draupadi, famed far and wide for her beauty and accomplishments, was going to choose a hero.

At a Svayamvara there was always a great feat of arms or something of the kind. On this occasion, a mark in the form of a fish was set up high in the sky; under that fish was a wheel with a hole in the centre, continually turning round, and beneath was a tub of water. A man looking at the reflection of the fish in the tub of water was asked to send an arrow and hit the eye of the fish through the Chakra or wheel, and he who succeeded would be married to the princess. Now, there came kings and princes from different parts of India, all anxious to win the hand of the princess, and one after another they tried their skill, and every one of them failed to hit the mark.

You know, there are four castes in India: the highest caste is that of the hereditary priest, the Brahmana; next is the caste of the Kshatriya, composed of kings and fighters; next, the Vaishyas, the traders or businessmen, and then Shudras, the servants. Now, this princess was, of course, a Kshatriya, one of the second caste.

When all those princes failed in hitting the mark, then the son of King Drupada rose up in the midst of the court and said: 'The Kshatriya, the king caste has failed; now the contest is open to the other castes. Let a Brahmana, even a Shudra, take part in it; whosoever hits the mark, marries Draupadi.'

Among the Brahmanas were seated the five Pandava brothers. Arjuna, the third brother, was the hero of the bow. He arose and stepped forward. Now, Brahmanas as a caste are very quiet and rather timid people. According to the law, they must not touch a warlike weapon, they must not wield a sword, they must not go into any enterprise that is dangerous. Their life is one of contemplation, study, and control of the inner nature. Judge, therefore, how quiet and peaceable a people they are. When the Brahmanas saw this man get up, they thought this man was going to bring the wrath of the Kshatriyas upon them, and that they would all be killed. So they tried to dissuade him, but Arjuna did not listen to them, because he was a soldier. He lifted the bow in his hand, strung it without any effort, and drawing it, sent the arrow right through the wheel and hit the eye of the fish.

Then there was great jubilation. Draupadi, the princess, approached Arjuna and threw the beautiful garland of flowers over his head. But there arose a great cry among the princes, who could not bear the idea that this beautiful princess who was a Kshatriya should be won by a poor Brahmana, from among this huge assembly of kings and princes. So, they wanted to fight Arjuna and snatch her from him by force. The brothers had a tremendous fight with the warriors, but held their own, and carried off the bride in triumph.

The five brothers now returned home to Kunti with the princess. Brahmanas have to live by begging. So they, who lived as Brahmanas, used to go out, and what they got by begging they brought home and the mother divided it among them. Thus the five brothers, with the princess, came to the cottage where the mother lived. They shouted out to her jocosely, 'Mother, we have brought home a most wonderful alms today.'

The mother replied, 'Enjoy it in common, all of you, my children.'

Then the mother seeing the princess, exclaimed, 'Oh! what have I said! It is a girl!'

But what could be done! The mother's word was spoken once for all. It must not be disregarded. The mother's words must be fulfilled. She could not be made to utter an untruth, as she never had done so. So Draupadi became the common wife of all the five brothers.

Now, you know, in every society there are stages of development. Behind this epic there is a wonderful glimpse of the ancient historic times. The author of the poem mentions the fact of the five brothers marrying the same woman, but he tries to gloss it over, to find an excuse and a cause for such an act; it was the mother's command, the mother sanctioned this strange betrothal, and so on. You know, in every nation there has been a certain stage in society that allowed polyandry—all the brothers of a family would marry one wife in common. Now, this was evidently a glimpse of the past polyandrous stage.

In the meantime, the brother of the princess was perplexed in his mind and thought: 'Who are these people? Who is this man whom my sister is going to marry? They have not any chariots, horses, or anything. Why, they go on foot!' So he had followed them at a distance, and at night overheard their conversation and became fully convinced that they were really Kshatriyas. Then King Drupada came to know who they were and was greatly delighted.

Though at first much objection was raised, it was declared by Vyasa that such a marriage was allowable for these princes, and it was permitted. So the king Drupada had to yield to this polyandrous marriage, and the princess was married to the five sons of Pandu.

Then the Pandavas lived in peace and prosperity and became more powerful every day. Though Duryodhana and his party conceived of fresh plots to destroy them, King Dhritarashtra was prevailed upon by the wise counsels of the elders to make peace with the Pandavas; and so he invited them home amidst the rejoicings of the people and gave them half of the kingdom. Then, the five brothers built for themselves a beautiful city, called Indraprastha, and extended their dominions, laying all the people under tribute to them.

Then the eldest, Yudhishthira, in order to declare himself emperor over all the kings of ancient India, decided to perform a Rajasuya Yajna, or Imperial Sacrifice, in which the conquered kings would have to come with tribute and swear allegiance, and help the performance of the sacrifice by personal services. Sri Krishna, who had become their friend and a relative, came to them and approved of the idea. But there was one obstacle to its performance. A king, Jarasandha by name, who intended to offer a sacrifice of a hundred kings, had eighty-six of them kept as captives with him. Sri Krishna counselled an attack on Jarasandha. So he, Bhima, and Arjuna challenged the king, who accepted the challenge and was finally conquered by Bhima after fourteen days' continuous wrestling. The captive kings were then set free.

Then the four younger brothers went out with armies on a conquering expedition, each in a different direction, and brought all the kings under subjection to Yudhishthira. Returning, they laid all the vast wealth they secured at the feet of the eldest brother to meet the expenses of the great sacrifice.

So, to this Rajasuya sacrifice all the liberated kings came, along with those conquered by the brothers, and rendered homage to Yudhishthira. King Dhritarashtra and his sons were also invited to come and take a share in the performance of the sacrifice. At the conclusion of the sacrifice, Yudhishthira was crowned emperor, and declared as lord paramount. This was the sowing of the future feud. Duryodhana came back from the sacrifice filled with jealousy against Yudhishthira, as their sovereignty and vast splendour and wealth were more than he could bear; and so he devised plans to effect their fall by guile, as he knew that to overcome them by force was beyond his power.

This king, Yudhishthira, had the love of gambling, and he was challenged at an evil hour to play dice with Shakuni, the crafty gambler and the evil genius of Duryodhana. In ancient India, if a man of the military caste was challenged to fight, he must at any price accept the challenge to uphold his honour. And if he was challenged to play dice, it was a point of honour to play, and dishonourable to decline the challenge. King Yudhishthira, says the Epic, was the incarnation of all virtues. Even he, the great sage-king, had to accept the challenge. Shakuni and his party had made false dice. So Yudhishthira lost game after game, and stung with his losses, he went on with the fatal game, staking everything he had, and losing all, until all his possessions, his kingdom and everything, were lost. The last stage came when, under further challenge, he had no other resources left but to stake his brothers, and then himself, and last of all, the fair Draupadi, and lost all. Now they were completely at the mercy of the Kauravas, who cast all sorts of insults upon them, and subjected Draupadi to the most inhuman treatment.

At last through the intervention of the blind king, they got their liberty, and were asked to return home and rule their kingdom. But Duryodhana saw the danger and forced his father to allow one more throw of the dice in which the party which would lose, should retire to the forests for twelve years, and then live unrecognised in a city for one year; but if they were found out, the same term of exile should have to be undergone once again and then only the kingdom was to be restored to the exiled. This last game also Yudhishthira lost, and the five Pandava brothers retired to the forests with Draupadi, as homeless exiles. They lived in the forests and mountains for twelve years. There they performed many deeds of virtue and valour, and would go out now and then on a long round of pilgrimages, visiting many holy places. That part of the poem is very interesting and instructive, and various are the incidents, tales, and legends with which this part of the book is replete. There are in it beautiful and sublime stories of ancient India, religious and philosophical. Great sages came to see the brothers in their exile and narrated to them many telling stories of ancient India, so as to make them bear lightly the burden of their exile. One only I will relate to you here.

There was a king called Ashvapati. The king had a daughter, who was so good and beautiful that she was called Savitri, which is the name of a sacred prayer of the Hindus. When Savitri grew old enough, her father asked her to choose a husband for herself. These ancient Indian princesses were very independent, you see, and chose their own princely suitors.

Savitri consented and travelled in distant regions, mounted in a golden chariot, with her guards and aged courtiers to whom her father entrusted her, stopping at different courts, and seeing different princes, but not one of them could win the heart of Savitri. They came at last to a holy hermitage in one of those forests that in ancient India were reserved for animals, and where no animals were allowed to be killed. The animals lost the fear of man—even the fish in the lakes came and took food out of the hand. For thousands of years no one had killed anything therein. The sages and the aged went there to live among the deer and the birds. Even criminals were safe there. When a man got tired of life, he would go to the forest; and in the company of sages, talking of religion and meditating thereon, he passed the remainder of his life.

Now it happened that there was a king, Dyumatsena, who was defeated by his enemies and was deprived of his kingdom when he was struck with age and had lost his sight. This poor, old, blind king, with his queen and his son, took refuge in the forest and passed his life in rigid penance. The boy's name was Satyavan.

It came to pass that after having visited all the different royal courts, Savitri at last came to this hermitage, or holy place. Not even the greatest king could pass by the hermitages, or ashramas as they were called, without going to pay homage to the sages, for such honour and respect was felt for these holy men. The greatest emperor of India would be only too glad to trace his descent to some sage who lived in a forest, subsisting on roots and fruits, and clad in rags. We are all children of sages. That is the respect that is paid to religion. So, even kings, when they pass by the hermitages, feel honoured to go in and pay their respects to the sages. If they approach on horseback, they descend and walk as they advance towards them. If they arrive in a chariot, chariot and armour must be left outside when they enter. No fighting man can enter unless he comes in the manner of a religious man, quiet and gentle.

So Savitri came to this hermitage and saw there Satyavan, the hermit's son, and her heart was conquered. She had escaped all the princes of the palaces and the courts, but here in the forest-refuge of the King Dyumatsena, his son, Satyavan, stole her heart.

When Savitri returned to her father's house, he asked

her, 'Savitri, dear daughter, speak. Did you see anybody whom you would like to marry?'

Then softly with blushes, said Savitri, 'Yes, father.'

'What is the name of the prince?'

'He is no prince, but the son of King Dyumatsena who has lost his kingdom—a prince without a patrimony, who lives a monastic life, the life of a sannyasin in a forest, collecting roots and herbs, helping and feeding his old father and mother, who live in a cottage.'

On hearing this the father consulted the Sage Narada, who happened to be then present there, and he declared it was the most ill-omened choice that was ever made. The king then asked him to explain why it was so.

And Narada said, 'Within twelve months from this time the young man will die.'

Then the king started with terror, and spoke, 'Savitri, this young man is going to die in twelve months, and you will become a widow; think of that! Desist from your choice, my child, you shall never be married to a short-lived and fated bridegroom.'

'Never mind, father; do not ask me to marry another person and sacrifice the chastity of mind, for I love and have accepted in my mind that good and brave Satyavan only as my husband. A maiden chooses only once, and she never departs from her troth.'

When the king found that Savitri was resolute in mind and heart, he complied. Then Savitri married prince Satyavan, and she quietly went from the palace of her father into the forest, to live with her chosen husband and help her husband's parents.

Now, though Savitri knew the exact date when Satyavan was to die, she kept it hidden from him. Daily he went into the depths of the forests, collected fruits and flowers, gathered faggots, and then came back to the cottage, and she cooked the meals and helped the old people. Thus their lives went on until the fatal day came near, and three short days remained only. She took a severe vow of three nights' penance and holy fasts, and kept her hard vigils. Savitri spent sorrowful and sleepless nights with fervent prayers and unseen tears, till the dreaded morning dawned.

That day Savitri could not bear him out of her sight, even for a moment. She begged permission from his parents to accompany her husband, when he went to gather the usual herbs and fuel, and gaining their consent she went. Suddenly, in faltering accents, he complained to his wife of feeling faint, 'My head is dizzy, and my senses reel, dear Savitri, I feel sleep stealing over me; let me rest beside thee for a while.' In fear and trembling she replied, 'Come, lay your head upon my lap, my dearest lord.' And he laid his burning head in the lap of his wife, and ere long sighed and expired.

Clasping him to her, her eyes flowing with tears, there she sat in the lonesome forest, until the emissaries of Death approached to take away the soul of Satyavan. But they could not come near to the place where Savitri sat with the dead body of her husband, his head resting in her lap. There was a zone of fire surrounding her, and not one of the emissaries of Death could come within it. They all fled back from it, returned to King Yama, the God of Death, and told him why they could not obtain the soul of this man.

Then came Yama, the God of Death, the Judge of the dead. He was the first man that died—the first man that died on earth—and he had become the presiding deity over all those that die. He judges whether, after a man has died, he is to be punished or rewarded. So he came himself. Of course, he could go inside that charmed circle, as he was a god.

When he came to Savitri, he said, 'Daughter, give up this dead body, for know, death is the fate of mortals, and I am the first of mortals who died. Since then, everyone has had to die. Death is the fate of man.'

Thus told, Savitri walked off, and Yama drew the soul out. Yama having possessed himself of the soul of the young man proceeded on his way. Before he had gone far, he heard footfalls upon the dry leaves.

He turned back. 'Savitri, daughter, why are you following me? This is the fate of all mortals.'

'I am not following thee, Father,' replied Savitri, 'but this is, also, the fate of woman, she follows where her love takes her, and the Eternal Law separates not loving man and faithful wife.'

Then said the God of Death, 'Ask for any boon, except the life of your husband.'

'If thou art pleased to grant a boon, O Lord of Death, I ask that my father-in-law may be cured of his blindness and made happy.'

'Let thy pious wish be granted, duteous daughter.'

And then the King of Death travelled on with the soul of Satyavan. Again the same footfall was heard from behind. He looked round. 'Savitri, my daughter, you are still following me?'

'Yes, my Father; I cannot help doing so; I am trying all the time to go back, but the mind goes after my husband and the body follows. The soul has already gone, for in that soul is also mine; and when you take the soul, the body follows, does it not?'

'Pleased am I with your words, fair Savitri. Ask yet another boon of me, but it must not be the life of your husband.' 'Let my father-in-law regain his lost wealth and kingdom, Father, if thou art pleased to grant another supplication.'

'Loving daughter,' Yama answered, 'this boon I now bestow; but return home, for living mortal cannot go with King Yama.'

And then Yama pursued his way. But Savitri, meek and faithful, still followed her departed husband. Yama again turned back. 'Noble Savitri, follow not in hopeless woe.'

'I cannot choose but follow where thou takest my beloved one.'

'Then suppose, Savitri, that your husband was a sinner and has to go to hell. In that case goes Savitri with the one she loves?'

'Glad am I to follow where he goes, be it life or death, heaven or hell,' said the loving wife. 'Blessed are your words, my child, pleased am I with you, ask yet another boon, but the dead come not to life again.'

'Since you so permit me, then, let the imperial line of my father-in-law be not destroyed; let his kingdom descend to Satyavan's sons.'

And then the God of Death smiled. 'My daughter, thou shalt have thy desire now: here is the soul of thy husband, he shall live again. He shall live to be a father and thy children also shall reign in due course. Return home. Love has conquered Death! Woman never loved like thee, and thou art the proof that even I, the God of Death, am powerless against the power of the true love that abideth!'

This is the story of Savitri, and every girl in India must aspire to be like Savitri, whose love could not be conquered by death, and who through this tremendous love snatched back from even Yama, the soul of her husband.

The book is full of hundreds of beautiful episodes like

14

this. I began by telling you that the Mahabharata is one of the greatest books in the world and consists of about a hundred thousand verses in eighteen Parvans, or volumes. To return to our main story. We left the Pandava brothers in exile. Even there they were not allowed to remain unmolested from the evil plots of Duryodhana; but all of them were futile.

A story of their forest life, I shall tell you here. One day the brothers became thirsty in the forest. Yudhishthira bade his brother, Nakula, go and fetch water. He quickly proceeded towards the place where there was water and soon came to a crystal lake, and was about to drink of it, when he heard a voice utter these words: 'Stop, O child. First answer my questions and then drink of this water.' But Nakula, who was exceedingly thirsty, disregarded these words, drank of the water, and having drunk of it, dropped down dead.

As Nakula did not return, King Yudhishthira told Sahadeva to seek his brother and bring back water with him. So Sahadeva proceeded to the lake and beheld his brother lying dead. Afflicted at the death of his brother and suffering severely from thirst, he went towards the water, when the same words were heard by him: 'O child, first answer my questions and then drink of the water.' He also disregarded these words, and having satisfied his thirst, dropped down dead. Subsequently Arjuna and Bhima were sent, one after the other, on a similar quest; but neither returned, having drunk of the lake and dropped down dead. Then Yudhishthira rose up to go in search of his brothers.

At length, he came to the beautiful lake and saw his brothers lying dead. His heart was full of grief at the sight, and he began to lament. Suddenly he heard the same voice saying, 'Do not, O child, act rashly. I am a

Yaksha living as a crane on tiny fish. It is by me that thy younger brothers have been brought under the sway of the Lord of departed spirits. If thou, O Prince, answer not the questions put by me, even thou shalt number the fifth corpse. Having answered my questions first, do thou, O Kunti's son, drink and carry away as much as thou requirest.'

Yudhishthira replied, 'I shall answer thy questions according to my intelligence. Do thou ask me!'

The Yaksha then asked him several questions, all of which Yudhishthira answered satisfactorily.

One of the questions was: 'What is the most wonderful fact in this world?'

'We see our fellow-beings every moment falling off around us; but those that are left behind think that they will never die. This is the most curious fact: in face of death, none believes he will die!'

Another question was: 'What is the path of knowing the secret of religion?'

And Yudhishthira answered, 'By argument nothing can be settled; doctrines there are many; various are the scriptures, one part contradicting the other. There are not two sages who do not differ in their opinions. The secret of religion is buried deep, as it were, in dark caves. So the path to be followed is that which the great ones have trodden.'

Then the Yaksha said, 'I am pleased. I am Dharma, the God of Justice in the form of a crane. I came to test you. Now, your brothers, see, not one of them is dead. It is all my magic. Since abstention from injury is regarded by thee as higher than both profit and pleasure, therefore, let all thy brothers live, O bull of the Bharata race.' And at these words of the Yaksha, the Pandavas rose up.

Here is a glimpse of the nature of King Yudhishthira. We find by his answers that he was more of a philosopher, more of a yogi, than a king.

Now, as the thirteenth year of the exile was drawing nigh, the Yaksha bade them go to Virata's kingdom and live there in such disguises as they would think best.

So, after the term of the twelve years' exile had expired, they went to the kingdom of Virata in different disguises to spend the remaining one year in concealment, and entered into menial service in the king's household. Thus Yudhishthira became a Brahmana courtier of the king, as one skilled in dice; Bhima was appointed a cook; Arjuna, dressed as a eunuch, was made a teacher of dancing and music to Uttara, the princess, and remained in the inner apartments of the king; Nakula became the keeper of the king's horses; and Sahadeva got the charge of the cows; and Draupadi, disguised as a waiting-woman was also admitted into the queen's household. Thus concealing their identity the Pandava brothers safely spent a year, and the search of Duryodhana to find them out was of no avail. They were only discovered just when the year was out.

Then Yudhishthira sent an ambassador to Dhritarashtra and demanded that half of the kingdom should, as their share, be restored to them. But Duryodhana hated his cousins and would not consent to their legitimate demands. They were even willing to accept a single province, nay, even five villages. But the headstrong Duryodhana declared that he would not yield without fight even as much land as a needle's point would hold. Dhritarashtra pleaded again and again for peace, but all in vain. Krishna also went and tried to avert the impending war and death of kinsmen, so did the wise elders of the royal court; but all negotiations for a peaceful partition of the kingdom were futile. So, at last, preparations were made on both sides for war, and all the warlike nations took part in it.

The old Indian customs of the Kshatriyas were observed in it. Duryodhana took one side, Yudhishthira, the other. From Yudhishthira messengers were at once sent to all the surrounding kings, entreating their alliance, since honourable men would grant the request that first reached them. So, warriors from all parts assembled to espouse the cause of either the Pandavas or the Kurus according to the precedence of their requests; and thus one brother joined this side, and the other that side, the father on one side, and the son on the other. The most curious thing was the code of war of those days; as soon as the battle for the day ceased and evening came, the opposing parties were good friends, even going to each other's tents; however, when the morning came, again they proceeded to fight each other. That was the strange trait that the Hindus carried down to the time of the Mohammedan invasion.

Then again, a man on horseback must not strike one on foot; must not poison the weapon; must not vanquish the enemy in any unequal fight, or by dishonesty; and must never take undue advantage of the other, and so on. If any deviated from these rules he would be covered with dishonour and shunned. The Kshatriyas were trained in that way. And when the foreign invasion came from Central Asia, the Hindus treated the invaders in the selfsame way. They defeated them several times, and on as many occasions sent them back to their homes with presents, etc. The code laid down was that they must not usurp anybody's country; and when a man was beaten he must be sent back to his country with due regard to his position.

The Mohammedan conquerors treated the Hindu kings differently, and when they got them once, they destroyed them without remorse.

Mind you, in those days—in the times of our story, the poem says—the science of arms was not the mere use of bows and arrows at all; it was magic archery in which the use of Mantras, concentration, etc., played a prominent part. One man could fight millions of men and burn them at will. He could send one arrow, and it would rain thousands of arrows and thunder; he could make anything burn, and so on—it was all divine magic. One fact is curious in both these poems—the Ramayana and the Mahabharata—along with these magic arrows and all these things going on, you see the cannon already in use. The cannon is an old, old thing, used by the Chinese and the Hindus. Upon the walls of the cities were hundreds of curious weapons made of hollow iron tubes, which filled with powder and ball would kill hundreds of men. The people believed that the Chinese, by magic, put the devil inside a hollow iron tube, and when they applied a little fire to a hole, the devil came out with a terrific noise and killed many people.

So in those old days, they used to fight with magic arrows. One man would be able to fight millions of others. They had their military arrangements and tactics: there were the foot soldiers, termed the Pada; then the cavalry, Turaga; and two other divisions which the moderns have lost and given up—there was the elephant corps—hundreds and hundreds of elephants, with men on their backs, formed into regiments and protected with huge sheets of iron mail; and these elephants would bear down upon a mass of the enemy—then, there were the chariots, of course (you have all seen pictures of those old chariots, they were used in every country). These were the four divisions of the army in those old days.

Now, both parties alike wished to secure the alliance of Krishna. But he declined to take an active part and fight in the war, but offered himself as charioteer to Arjuna, and as the friend and counsellor of the Pandavas, while to Duryodhana he gave his army of mighty solders.

Then was fought on the vast plain of Kurukshetra the great battle in which Bhisma, Drona, Karna, and the brothers of Duryodhana with the kinsmen on both sides and thousands of other heroes fell. The war lasted eighteen days. Indeed, out of the eighteen Akshauhinis of soldiers very few men were left. The death of Duryodhana ended the war in favour of the Pandavas. It was followed by the lament of Gandhari, the queen, and the widowed women, and the funerals of the deceased warriors.

The greatest incident of the war was the marvellous and immortal poem of the Gita, the Song Celestial. It is the popular scripture of India and the loftiest of all teachings. It consists of a dialogue held by Arjuna with Krishna, just before the commencement of the fight on the battle-field of Kurukshetra. I would advise those of you who have not read that book to read it. If you only knew how much it has influenced your own country even! If you want to know the source of Emerson's inspiration, it is this book, the Gita. He went to see Carlyle, and Carlyle made him a present of the Gita; and that little book is responsible for the Concord Movement. All the broad movements in America, in one way or other, are indebted to the Concord party.

The central figure of the Gita is Krishna. As you worship Jesus of Nazareth as God come down as man, so the Hindus worship many Incarnations of God. They believe in not one or two only, but in many, who have come down from time to time, according to the needs of the world, for the preservation of Dharma and destruction of wickedness. Each sect has one, and Krishna is one of them. Krishna, perhaps, has a larger number of followers in India than any other Incarnation of God. His followers hold that he was the most perfect of those Incarnations. Why?

'Because,' they say, 'look at Buddha and other Incarnations; they were only monks, and they had no sympathy for married people. How could they have? But look at Krishna; he was great as a son, as a king, as a father, and all through his life he practised the marvellous teachings which he preached.'

'He who in the midst of the greatest activity finds the sweetest peace, and in the midst of the greatest calmness is most active, he has known the secret of life.'

Krishna shows the way how to do this—by being non-attached: do everything but do not get identified with anything. You are the soul, the pure, the free, all the time; you are the Witness. Our misery comes, not from work, but by our getting attached to something. Take for instance, money: money is a great thing to have, earn it, says Krishna; struggle hard to get money, but don't get attached to it. So with children, with wife, husband, relatives, fame, everything; you have no need to shun them, only don't get attached. There is only one attachment and that belongs to the Lord, and to none other. Work for them, love them, do good to them, sacrifice a hundred lives, if need be, for them, but never be attached. His own life was the exact exemplification of that.

Remember that the book which delineates the life of Krishna is several thousand years old, and some parts of his life are very similar to those of Jesus of Nazareth. Krishna was of royal birth; there was a tyrant king, called

Kamsa, and there was a prophecy that one would be born of such and such a family, who would be king. So Kamsa ordered all the male children to be massacred. The father and mother of Krishna were cast by King Kamsa into prison, where the child was born.

A light suddenly shone in the prison and the child spoke saying, 'I am the Light of the world, born for the good of the world.'

You find Krishna again symbolically represented with cows—'The Great Cowherd' as he is called. Sages affirmed that God Himself was born, and they went to pay him homage. In other parts of the story, the similarity between the two does not continue.

Sri Krishna conquered this tyrant Kamsa, but he never thought of accepting or occupying the throne himself. He had nothing to do with that. He had done his duty and there it ended.

After the conclusion of the Kurukshetra War, the great warrior and venerable grandsire, Bhishma, who fought ten days out of the eighteen days' battle, still lay on his deathbed and gave instructions to Yudhishthira on various subjects, such as the duties of the king, the duties of the four castes, the four stages of life, the laws of marriage, the bestowing of gifts, etc., basing them on the teachings of the ancient sages. He explained Sankhya philosophy and yoga philosophy and narrated numerous tales and traditions about saints and gods and kings. These teachings occupy nearly one-fourth of the entire work and form an invaluable storehouse of Hindus laws and moral codes. Yudhishthira had in the meantime been crowned king. But the awful bloodshed and extinction of superiors and relatives weighed heavily on his mind; and then, under the advice of Vyasa, he performed the Ashvamedha sacrifice.

After the war, for fifteen years Dhritarashtra dwelt in peace and honour, obeyed by Yudhishthira and his brothers. Then the aged monarch leaving Yudhishthira on the throne, retired to the forest with his devoted wife and Kunti, the mother of the Pandava brothers, to pass his last days in asceticism.

Thirty-six years had now passed since Yudhishthira regained his empire. Then came to him the news that Krishna had left his mortal body. Krishna, the sage, his friend, his prophet, his counsellor, had departed. Arjuna hastened to Dwaraka and came back only to confirm the sad news that Krishna and the Yadavas were all dead. Then the king and the other brothers, overcome with sorrow, declared that the time for them to go, too, had arrived. So they cast off the burden of royalty, placed Parikshit, the grandson of Arjuna, on the throne, and retired to the Himalayas, on the Great Journey, the Mahaprasthana.

This was a peculiar form of Sannyasa. It was a custom for old kings to become sannyasins. In ancient India, when men became very old, they would give up everything. So did the kings. When a man did not want to live any more, then he went towards the Himalayas, without eating or drinking and walked on and on till the body failed. All the time thinking of God, he just marched on till the body gave way.

Then came the gods, the sages, and they told King Yudhishthira that he should go and reach heaven. To go to heaven one has to cross the highest peaks of the Himalayas. Beyond the Himalayas is Mount Meru. On the top of Mount Meru is heaven. None ever went there in this body. There the gods reside. And Yudhishthira was called upon by the gods to go there.

So the five brothers and their wife clad themselves

in robes of bark, and set out on their journey. On the way, they were followed by a dog. On and on they went, and they turned their weary feet northward to where the Himalayas lifts his lofty peaks, and they saw the mighty Mount Meru in front of them. Silently they walked on in the snow, until suddenly the queen fell, to rise no more.

To Yudhishthira who was leading the way, Bhima, one of the brothers said, 'Behold, O King, the queen has fallen.'

The king shed tears, but he did not look back. 'We are going to meet Krishna,' he says.

'No time to look back. March on.' After a while, again Bhima said, 'Behold, our brother, Sahadeva has fallen.'

The king shed tears; but paused not. 'March on,' he cried.

One after the other, in the cold and snow, all the four brothers dropped down, but unshaken, though alone, the king advanced onward. Looking behind, he saw the faithful dog was still following him. And so the king and the dog went on, through snow and ice, over hill and dale, climbing higher and higher, till they reached Mount Meru; and there they began to hear the chimes of heaven, and celestial flowers were showered upon the virtuous king by the gods.

Then descended the chariot of the gods, and Indra prayed him, 'Ascend in this chariot, greatest of mortals: thou that alone art given to enter heaven without changing the mortal body.' But no, that Yudhishthira would not do without his devoted brothers and his queen; then Indra explained to him that the brothers had already gone thither before him.

And Yudhishthira looked around and said to his dog, 'Get into the chariot, child.'

The god stood aghast. 'What! The dog?' he cried. 'Do thou cast off this dog! The dog goeth not to heaven! Great King, what dost thou mean? Art thou mad? Thou, the most virtuous of the human race, thou only canst go to heaven in thy body.'

'But he has been my devoted companion through the snow and ice. When all my brothers were dead, my queen dead, he alone never left me. How can I leave him now?'

'There is no place in heaven for men with dogs. He has to be left behind. There is nothing unrighteous in this.'

'I do not go to heaven,' replied the king, 'without this dog. I shall never give up such a one who has taken refuge with me, until my own life is at an end. I shall never swerve from righteousness, nay, not even for the joys of heaven or the urging of a god.'

'Then,' said Indra, 'on one condition the dog goes to heaven. You have been the most virtuous of mortals and he has been a dog, killing and eating animals; he is sinful, hunting, and taking other lives. You can exchange heaven with him.'

'Agreed,' says the king. 'Let the dog go to heaven.'

At once, the scene changed. Hearing these noble words of Yudhishthira, the dog revealed himself as Dharma; the dog was no other than Yama, the Lord of Death and Justice.

And Dharma exclaimed, 'Behold, O King, no man was ever so unselfish as thou, willing to exchange heaven with a little dog, and for his sake disclaiming all his virtues and ready to go to hell even for him. Thou art well born, O King of kings. Thou hast compassion for all creatures, O Bharata, of which this is a bright example. Hence, regions of undying felicity are thine! Thou has won them, O King, and thine is a celestial and high goal.'

Then Yudhishthira, with Indra, Dharma, and other gods, proceeds to heaven in a celestial car. He undergoes some trials, bathes in the celestial Ganga, and assumes a celestial body. He meets his brothers who are now immortals, and all at last is bliss.

Thus ends the story of the Mahabharata, setting forth in a sublime poem the triumph of virtue and the defeat of vice.

In speaking of the Mahabharata to you, it is simply impossible for me to present the unending array of the grand and majestic characters of the mighty heroes depicted by the genius and master-mind of Vyasa. The internal conflicts between righteousness and filial affection in the mind of the god-fearing, yet feeble, old, blind King Dhritarashtra; the majestic character of the grandsire Bhishma; the noble and virtuous character of the royal Yudhishthira, and of the other four brothers, as mighty in valour as in devotion and loyalty; the peerless character of Krishna, unsurpassed in human wisdom; and not less brilliant, the characters of the women—the stately queen Gandhari, the loving mother Kunti, the ever-devoted and all-suffering Draupadi—these and hundreds of other characters of this Epic and those of the Ramayana have been the cherished heritage of the whole Hindu world for the last several thousands of years and form the basis of their thoughts and of their moral and ethical ideas.

In fact, the Ramayana and the Mahabharata are the two encyclopaedias of the ancient Aryan life and wisdom, portraying an ideal civilisation which humanity has yet to aspire after. (CW, 4:78-101)

104. Real Prayer is Unconditional

We have heard it said that a great king once went into a forest and there met a sage. He talked with the sage a little and was very much pleased with his purity and wisdom. The king then wanted the sage to oblige him by receiving a present from him.

The sage refused to do so, saying, 'The fruits of the forest are enough food for me; the pure streams of water flowing down from the mountains give enough drink for me; the barks of the trees supply me with enough covering; and the caves of the mountains form my home. Why should I take any present from you or from anybody?'

The king said, 'Just to benefit me, sir, please take something from my hands and please come with me to the city and to my palace.'

After much persuasion, the sage at last consented to do as the king desired and went with him to his palace.

Before offering the gift to the sage, the king repeated his prayers, saying, 'Lord, give me more children; Lord, give me more wealth; Lord, give me more territory; Lord, keep my body in better health', and so on.

Before the king finished saying his prayer, the sage had got up and walked away from the room quietly.

At this the king became perplexed and began to follow him, crying aloud, 'Sir, you are going away, you have not received my gifts.'

The sage turned round to him and said, 'I do not beg of beggars. You are yourself nothing but a beggar, and how can you give me anything? I am no fool to think of taking anything from a beggar like you. Go away, do not follow me.' (CW, 3:87-88)

105. Judge Ye Not

We are always making this mistake in judging others; we are always inclined to think that our little mental universe is all that is; our ethics, our morality, our sense of duty, our sense of utility, are the only things that are worth having.

The other day when I was going to Europe, I was passing through Marseilles, where a bull-fight was being held. All the Englishmen in the steamer were mad with excitement, abusing and criticising the whole thing as cruel. When I reached England, I heard of a party of prize-fighters who had been to Paris, and were kicked out unceremoniously by the French, who thought prize-fighting very brutal.

When I hear these things in various countries, I begin to understand the marvellous saying of Christ: 'Judge not that ye be not judged.' The more we learn, the more we find out how ignorant we are, how multiform and multi-sided is this mind of man.

When I was a boy, I used to criticise the ascetic practices of my countrymen; great preachers in our own land have criticised them; the greatest man that was ever born, Buddha himself, criticised them. But all the same, as I am growing older, I feel that I have no right to judge. Sometimes I wish that, in spite of all their incongruities, I had one fragment of their power to do and to suffer. Often I think that my judgment and my criticism do not proceed from any dislike of torture, but from sheer cowardice—because I cannot do it—I dare not do it. (CW, 2:24-25)

106. A Calcutta Youth in Father-in-law's House

A youth of Calcutta once visited his father-in-law's place in a remote village far from the Ganga. There at dinner-time he found people waiting about with drums etc., and his mother-in-law insisted on his taking a little milk before sitting to dinner.

The son-in-law considered it might perhaps be a local custom which he had better obey; but no sooner had he taken a sip of the milk than the drums began to play all around and his mother-in-law, with tears of joy, placed her hand on his head and blessed him, saying, 'My son, you have really discharged the duties of a son today; look here, you have in your stomach the water of the Ganga, as you live on its banks, and in the milk there was the powdered bone of your deceased father-in-law; so by this act of yours his bones have reached the Ganga and his spirit has obtained all the merits thereof.' (CW, 7:309-10)